SABBATH Q[

In writing about the sabbath, I know ⌐ ⌐ ⌐⌐⌐⌐ ⌐⌐⌐. ⌐⌐ other books, I have pressed buttons of a vermilion hue, but this tends to the infra-red. By linking 'sabbath' and 'questions', in the eyes of many I will have put myself beyond the pale before I start. It will confirm what they have suspected for a long time: 'David Gay is an antinomian. Have nothing to do with him or his works'.

Well, I am more than happy to be accused of antinomianism for preaching the gospel with apostolic freeness. After all, Paul was accused of it (Rom. 3:5-8; 6:1). Consequently, I say to those who accuse me of antinomianism over the gospel: 'You fail to preach the gospel as it ought to be preached. You mix law and gospel'.

But what about my view of the law? I have made my position clear. I am anti-Reformed on the law. I do not accept Calvin's threefold use of the law. But to call me an antinomian for saying this is a mark of ignorance. Or worse! Read my works and see. Listen to my sermons. I am not anti-law. I am pro-gospel, pro-Christ – for justification, for assurance, for sanctification, for liberation, for glorification. Christ is all (Col. 3:11).

But what about the sabbath? This, of course, is the reddest of all red buttons. And I press it. I do so because a friend (who reads my works and hears me preach) asked for help because Iain Murray's book *Evangelical Holiness* raised problems for her, problems she could not answer. In writing something for her, it struck me it might help others. Hence this publication.

All I ask is that you read this work with an open Bible. Is it too much to ask that you start with an open mind? Above all, be a Berean: 'The Bereans... received the message with great eagerness and examined the Scriptures every day to see if what Paul said was true' (Acts 17:11).

Sabbath Questions

An open letter to Iain Murray

The law was given through Moses; grace and truth came through Jesus Christ

John 1:17

There remains, then, a sabbath rest for the people of God

Hebrews 4:9

David H.J.Gay

BRACHUS

BRACHUS 2014
davidhjgay@googlemail.com

Scripture quotations come from a variety of versions

Contents

Note to the reader

In writing about the sabbath, I know I am taking a huge risk. In other books, I have pressed buttons of a vermilion hue, but this tends to the infra-red. By linking 'sabbath' and 'questions', in the eyes of many I will have put myself beyond the pale before I start. It will confirm what they have suspected for a long time: 'David Gay is an antinomian. Have nothing to do with him or his works'.

Well, I am more than happy to be accused of antinomianism for preaching the gospel with apostolic freeness. After all, Paul was accused of it (Rom. 3:5-8; 6:1). Consequently, I say to those who accuse me of antinomianism over the gospel: 'You fail to preach the gospel as it ought to be preached. You mix law and gospel'.

But what about my view of the law? I have made my position clear. I am anti-Reformed on the law. I do not accept Calvin's threefold use of the law. But to call me an antinomian for saying this is a mark of ignorance. Or worse! Read my works and see. Listen to my sermons. I am not anti-law. I am pro-gospel, pro-Christ – for justification, for assurance, for sanctification, for liberation, for glorification. Christ is all (Col. 3:11).

But what about the sabbath? This, of course, is the reddest of all red buttons. And I press it. I do so because a friend (who reads my works and hears me preach) asked for help because Iain Murray's book *Evangelical Holiness* raised problems for her, problems she could not answer. In writing something for her, it struck me it might help others. Hence this publication. In the main, I respond to Iain under his own headings. This means that some of the material gets more than one reference, but I accept this since I want to make each section as complete as possible in itself.

All I ask is that you read this work with an open Bible. Is it too much to ask that you start with an open mind? Above all, be a Berean: 'The Bereans... received the message with great eagerness and examined the Scriptures every day to see if what Paul said was true' (Acts 17:11).

As for my own observance of the Lord's day, I say two things.[1] Although I am not a sabbatarian,[2] I have friends who are sure that I

---

[1] When I talk about 'the Lord's day', I mean the first day of the week. But, unlike sabbatarians, I do not call this 'the Christian sabbath'.

am. And they have a point. Having been born in the UK in 1940, I have puritanical and sabbatarian DNA. Frankly, like most UK citizens of my age, I am genetically sabbatarian. Indeed, for the first three decades of my walk with Christ I was a typical Reformed-sabbatarian. It was preaching through Hebrews which began the change in my view of the law – at that stage, the sabbath in particular. Preaching through Galatians confirmed it. Secondly, although it will sound like bragging, over the years I have out-gunned most sabbatarians I know. They have done things on the Lord's day that I would never do. They might call me an antinomian, but I say they are hypocrites: they profess to be sabbatarians, but they have invented a host of ways to get round the sabbath's observance. Not to put too fine a point on it, they get far too close for (their) comfort to Christ's stricture: 'The teachers of the law and the Pharisees sit in Moses' seat... But... they do not practice what they preach. They tie up heavy loads and put them on men's shoulders, but they themselves are not willing to lift a finger to move them' (Matt. 23:2-4). If it were not so serious, the machinations of the sabbatarians would be highly amusing. As it stands, they are often ludicrous. Read their books and see!

It appears as though I am trying to defend myself. Not at all! I only say this because a non-sabbatarian friend – one who is sure that I am a sabbatarian – has warned me that unless I make my position clear right from the start, nobody will read my work. I feel the force of his words. Hence this opening note.

Finally, too often my sabbatarianism has been a matter of legal fear. And largely negative. I am not alone in having to confess this. My observance of the Lord's day, however, I want to be from the heart, and out of love for Christ, in the spirit of the new covenant.

But, as I say, this present volume is to do with the sabbath.

---

[2] When I talk about 'sabbatarians', I mean those who argue for observance of what they call 'the Christian sabbath', not the more-consistent sabbatarians (such as Seventh-Day Adventists or Baptists), although much of what I say is relevant to them.

Speaking the truth in love, we will in all things grow up into him who is the head, that is, Christ

Ephesians 4:15

My Letter

My letter to Iain

My dear Iain,[1]

I write to you about your work on the sabbath: 'Rest in God: The Fourth Commandment *is* for Today', in *Evangelical Holiness and other addresses*, The Banner of Truth Trust, Edinburgh, 2013, pp139-169.

While I consider this to be the best short (attempted) defence I have seen of the position that the Lord's day (Sunday) is the Christian sabbath, a day of obligatory observance for all men today, I strongly disagree with much of what you say, and I want to respond.

I am a Lord's day man. I am not a sabbatarian. I am convinced that the sabbath was from first to last entirely Jewish, an essential part of the old covenant, which was fulfilled, terminated, accomplished, abolished and rendered obsolete by Christ when he established the new covenant. Having set out my arguments on the law elsewhere,[2] I simply state here that sabbatarianism is Jewish, and was ended with Christ and the new covenant.

This, of course, is no trivial matter, a question of mere words. Was Calvin right with his threefold use of the law? I ask this because, as we both know, his teaching on the law has dominated Reformed and evangelical Christianity these past 450 years. You are convinced that Calvin was right. I am sure that on this vital matter Calvin was wrong. And the sabbath is but the tip of the iceberg in this debate over the law. To change the figure and mix my metaphors: in my experience, the sabbath is the reddest of all red buttons – press it and the heavens fall!

As a consequence, I respond to your work on the sabbath by way of an open letter, written with the wider public in mind. By no

---

[1] This is no affectation. Iain and I have been acquainted with each other for more than 50 years.
[2] In particular, in my *Christ is All: No Sanctification by the Law*, Brachus, Wilstead, 2013.

11

means do I include my full argument on the sabbath,[3] but I confine myself to certain salient points arising directly out of your work. Nothing, therefore, may be deduced from what I say in this book about my views on the Lord's day. Nothing! While I do not question that the Lord's day is a day of public assembly and worship for believers, and only for believers, I confine my remarks here entirely to the sabbath. The title says it all: 'Sabbath Questions'. I am talking about the sabbath, not the Lord's day, I stress. I know that you equate the two. I do not. I am sure that you, and the public, therefore, will not attribute views to me regarding the Lord's day until I have gone into print on it, as I hope to do. I say this for the benefit of all my friends, both 'antinomian' and 'law monger'.[4]

I write out of regard, respect and spiritual love for you as a brother in the Lord. But in tandem with that respect, I also write out of love for the truth, and a wish to do nothing but good in challenging your work in this public way. May God bless us both in this. In addition, may he bless all who read our respective works on this important question.

As for your Christian love to me, may I ask if you stand by your implication, if not assertion, in quotations from Robert Murray M'Cheyne and John Willison, that a non-sabbatarian like me cannot be 'a lively believer',[5] cannot be 'one who loves Christ', and cannot be 'living a holy life'?[6] Are you saying that, because I disagree with you over the sabbath, I 'discount [that is, disregard, ignore, disbelieve, write off] the ten commandments'?[7] Are you also saying, because I disagree with you and your

---

[3] For much more, see my *Sabbath Notes & Extracts*, Brachus, 2014.

[4] By 'law monger', I mean those who say that we must preach the law to sinners to bring them to Christ, stop preaching the law just as they are about to trust Christ alone for justification, and then immediately take them back under the law for sanctification. I also include those who do this in an incipient way. My short denial of it all can be found in 1 Cor. 2:2; 9:16; 2 Cor. 4:5. For a longer answer, see my *Christ* (*passim*).

[5] Although the talk is of the Lord's day, you mean the sabbath.

[6] Murray p164.

[7] If so, please read my works and listen to my sermons.

Reformed preparationism,[8] that I verge on being an antinomian, if not being one, and that I am hindering sinners in coming to Christ because I am acting 'contrary to biblical evangelism'?[9]

The truth is, as it stands, you are going much further than merely dismissing me as an antinomian. According to the extracts you approve of, you are saying that, because I am not a sabbatarian, I am not a believer at all! Do you stand by that?

If so, you are in danger of putting creed above life. In other words, if a man ticks the right boxes, he must be kosher. Yet when I read the apostle, I find that he knows his readers are elect because he sees the fruits of it in their lives (1 Thess. 1:4-10). And we have the plain words of Christ: 'By their fruit you will recognise them' (Matt. 7:16-20). 'By this all men will know that you are my disciples, if you love one another' (John 13:35).

Let me hasten to add that I am not playing 'the Spirit' (or 'the spirit') against 'the word',[10] but I am saying that you are in danger of staying with – or going back to – 'the letter', and playing down, if not ignoring, 'the Spirit' (Rom. 7:4-6; 2 Cor. 3:1-18). Sadly, as I will show, you have ended up in that tragic position.

Furthermore, let me say that I am fully persuaded that if a man loves Christ he will keep his commandments (John 13:34-35; 14:15,21,23-24; 15:10; Jas. 1:25; 2:12; 1 John 5:2-3; 2 John 6). But, of course, in the new covenant, these commandments are part of the law of Christ (1 Cor. 9:21; Gal. 6:2; 2 Pet. 3:2) for his new Israel (Gal. 6:16; Phil. 3:3), not the law of Moses (John 1:17). Not, I hasten to add, that the law of Christ is a mere set of rules. I will not expand on this vital point here,[11] but the law of Christ is an entirely new system, regime, principle, one which is radically different to the ambience of the law of Moses. It is, as I say, the law of 'the Spirit' as opposed to the killing 'letter' of Moses (Rom. 7:4-6; 2 Cor. 3:6-9; Gal. 2:19; 5:18). As the apostle told us plainly:

---

[8] That is, we must preach the law to sinners to prepare them for Christ, make them 'fit' for Christ, by bringing them to conviction of sin. Nothing but the law will do this. See my *Christ* pp51-61,127-140,348-358,420-430.

[9] Murray p166.

[10] See my *Christ* pp255-256.

[11] See my *Christ* pp211-278,481-527.

Through Christ Jesus the law of the Spirit of life set me free from the law of sin and death. For what the law was powerless to do in that it was weakened by the flesh, God did by sending his own Son in the likeness of sinful man to be a sin offering. And so he condemned sin in sinful man, in order that the righteous requirements of the law might be fully met in us, who do not live according to the flesh but according to the Spirit (Rom. 8:2-4).

The material point is this: I quite understand that you might say that I (and others like me) are wrong, misguided, or some such, but can you not allow that sincere believers might not be sabbatarian, and yet still be keeping the law of Christ, as they understand it? Or is the keeping of the Puritan sabbath (for that is what we are really talking about) the touchstone of genuine conversion, after all? If it is, it would be helpful if you said it straight out. Actually, it would be more than 'helpful'. Out of love for sinners in general, and in discharge of your responsibility before God (Ezek. 3:16-21; 33:1-9), you (and those who agree with you) ought to make the fact as widely known as possible – throughout the whole world – and do so in loud and unmistakable terms. You owe it, not only to me, but to every man, woman and child on the planet: unless men keep the Puritan sabbath, they will be damned!

If you were prepared to treat sabbath observance (as you understand it) as something 'indifferent' (Rom. 14:1 – 15:7; 1 Cor. 8:1-13; 10:23 – 11:1), and act in accordance with the apostle's principles as set out in those passages, I would, I hope, speak to you and try to show you the liberty we have in Christ, but, in the spirit of those passages, do it privately. But, of course, since sabbath observance is nothing less than the fourth commandment, and since you are convinced that obedience to the law of God is binding on all men, you (rightly, in your terms) *insist* on universal sabbath observance, particularly by believers. Accordingly, it is only right that I should respond in the spirit of Acts 15:10, and do so at the same level as your insistence on sabbath observance; namely, by publication of a book.

Let me say one thing more on this point. I agree with you to this extent: sabbath observance is not a thing indifferent. It is the fourth commandment, and as such is a vital part of the inflexible and inviolable law of God to all who are (or were) under it. And, with respect, that is why you need to be very sure that you really are secure in your attempted justification of changes to that law. Not only that. You need to be confident that God really will excuse you for any falling short of the command, especially when you employ Reformed schemes designed to evade the law. I say this for you, personally, and for all who read your book and try to adopt your principles.

Finally, as I am sure you understand, I do not engage with you in an arid point-scoring tourney; nor am I interested in a mere academic debate. As you yourself make clear, this is a life-and-death matter. Depending on your answer to my earlier questions, that 'death' might be eternal. Yes, it is that serious! I am wrestling, therefore, for the well-being of men, women and children. Not only that. In the ultimate, I am wrestling for their eternal welfare.

In addition, I want to do what I can to help believers enjoy the liberty they have in Christ, and not be 'burdened again by a yoke of slavery' by the law which the Jews found they could never keep (Acts 15:10; Gal. 5:1).

I say these things so that all who read my book may know where I am coming from, and what I am aiming for.

As always, I remain your brother in the Lord.

The Bereans... received the message with great eagerness and examined the Scriptures every day to see if what Paul said was true
Acts 17:11

My Comments on Murray's Work

You are sure that the sabbath is for mankind, all mankind, that its 'appointment' has 'universal significance', since 'the fourth commandment does not belong exclusively to the Jews'; the fourth commandment, being part of 'the moral law... has authority over Gentile as well as Jew'. Accordingly, all men are obliged to keep the sabbath, because 'to be "under law" is descriptive of all men by nature'.[1] 'The honouring of the fourth commandment has brought blessings to *nations*'. 'The inability of non-Christians to keep the Lord's day [in your terms, the sabbath][2] in no way lessens their responsibility to keep it. The obligation rests upon the eternal principles set out in the moral law.[3] Fallen man... is still held to account for the obedience which God requires... The moral law exists for all mankind'.[4]

All that is clear enough. May I ask you some questions about it?

The sabbath binding on all men?

Who was the first man to keep the sabbath? As recorded in Scripture, that is. Was it Adam? If he kept the sabbath, how do we know he did? Did any of the patriarchs keep the sabbath? Noah? Abraham? Which scripture tells us so? Again, who was the first man to break the sabbath? Which scripture tells us of the first case of it? Is there any record in Genesis of sabbath keeping among men? Is the sin of sabbath breaking ever mentioned in Genesis? If sabbath keeping was a creation ordinance, why do we not find at least one instance of its observance in Genesis? We read much about work and marriage in Genesis – why not the sabbath? We

---

[1] I agree that all men are 'under law' – if when you talk about non-Jews, you restrict 'law' to Rom. 2:14-15. But, of course you do not. You really mean 'the ten commandments' (Murray p149). I will return to your inexplicable mis-reading of Rom. 2:14-15.
[2] See below.
[3] In your terms, the ten commandments. See below.
[4] Murray pp147-149,157,162,166, emphasis mine.

read of many sins in Genesis – but never once of sabbath breaking. Why not?

We know the patriarchs sacrificed. We can, therefore, deduce that God conveyed his mind to the patriarchs regarding sacrifice. We know this because we see them sacrificing, repeatedly (Gen. 4:3-5; 8:20; 12:8; 13:18; 15:9-10,17; 22:13; 26:25; 33:20; 35:7 (reasonably assuming the references to an altar imply blood sacrifices).[5] Indeed, we have examples of God directly commanding such (Gen. 15:9; 22:2). Adam and Eve certainly learnt the principle from God's action in clothing them with animal skins (Gen. 3:21). No wonder, then, that Abel sacrificed. But where do we find any man keeping the sabbath before Exodus? The biblical silence speaks volumes! While in Genesis we have relative silence over a command to sacrifice, but examples of men sacrificing, we have neither command nor example of sabbath observance among men.

To move on: when God made his covenant with Noah (Gen. 8:20-9:17), he commanded him to 'be fruitful and multiply, and fill the earth', and he gave him dominion over the creatures – echoes of Genesis 1:28. But there was no mention of the sabbath. Indeed, in the light of the fact that the sabbath was the sign of the Mosaic covenant,[6] it is noteworthy that the sign of the Noahic covenant was the rainbow (Gen. 9:12-17), not the sabbath. Similarly, when God made his covenant with Abraham, he did not mention the sabbath, and the sign of the covenant was circumcision (Gen. 15:18-21; 17:1-14). So although Abraham obeyed God's commandments (Gen. 26:5), there is no evidence whatsoever that the sabbath was included in this. And, although I would not build my case upon it, it is worth mentioning that when Joseph exercised what amounted to absolute power in Egypt, he instituted laws which lasted far beyond his day, laws which took due account of current religious regulations in the land (Gen. 47:20-26), yet the sabbath is significant in his arrangements only by its absence.

What is more, if sabbath observance is a perpetual commandment for all the human race, why is there no New

---

[5] 'An altar is any structure upon which offerings such as sacrifices are made for religious purposes' (Wikipedia).
[6] See Appendix 2.

Testament teaching on the subject? We have a clear explanation of, say, civil government, and the necessity of obedience to it (Rom. 13:1-7; Tit. 3:1; 1 Pet. 2:11-17). The apostles instructed believers in this matter to put a stop to any foolish talk among them to the effect that, since they were now converted and liberated, they were free of the universal obligation to submit to rulers. 'The fact that you are believers', say the apostles, 'does not release you from the universal requirement to be submissive to civil authority'. So why do we not get the same for the sabbath, seeing sabbath breaking is attended with such awesome curses?[7] And, moreover, why is it that Paul, when writing so firmly against observance of days, including sabbaths,[8] does not, on account of the seriousness of breaking the sabbath, make it clear that, in delivering his dogmatic statements, he exempts sabbath observance by believers?

Iain, I am not arguing my case from silence, but just pointing out that if the apostle held your view, then he was being extremely cavalier in the way he wrote. After all, the churches of Rome, Galatia and Colosse were made up of Jewish and Gentile converts. Not only that. The teaching of the Judaisers – with their insistence that (Gentile) believers had to come under the law (Acts 15:1,5; Gal. 2:4; 5:12) – was rampant throughout the early churches. If not, why did Paul devote so much time and space to the law?[9]

And consider this: the apostle told some believers that observance of a sacred day was a thing indifferent (Rom. 14:5-12), rebuked others for 'observing special days' (Gal. 4:10), and forbad yet others to let anyone judge them 'with regard to... a sabbath day', teaching (reminding) them that it was 'a shadow' of Christ (Col. 2:16-17). Well? What of it? Notice what Paul did not do. He said nothing about the sabbath being an exception! But it is unthinkable that Paul would have failed to include an exception clause for the sabbath – if believers are to keep it, that is. Include?

---

[7] About which I will have more to say.

[8] Rom. 14:5-6; Gal. 4:10; Col. 2:16-17.

[9] Rom. 2:12-29; 4:13-17; 6:14 – 8:4; 9:30 – 10:5; 2 Cor. 3:1 – 4:6; Galatians; Eph. 2:8-18; Phil. 3:2-11; Col. 2:13-23; and so on. In addition, we have the letter to the Hebrews. By the way, the fact that the Judaisers were demanding Gentile submission to the law proves that the Gentiles never were under the law.

He should have been explicit. He should have put it up in lights. He would have done. You would have done. Look at the space you devote to the universal obligation of the sabbath, and the emphasis you lay upon it! So why did Paul omit this obvious necessity?

Pagans are obliged to keep the sabbath, you say. Very well. Are we really to believe that pagans who lived *before* the time of Christ knew they must rest from Friday sunset to Saturday sunset? and those who have lived *after* the time of Christ have known that they must keep it from Saturday midnight to Sunday midnight? Can you tell us of any pagan people who keep the sabbath? or feel guilty for not keeping it? By the way, who told the pagans of the change of day and its hours?

I move on to address what you call the 'complications' of sabbath observance.[10] You try to limit this by confining your remarks to believers. But, of course, on your own premise, this is impossible; pagans are obliged to keep the sabbath, you say. Now if sabbath observance is 'complicated' for believers, the mind boggles at the 'complications', and worse, that must arise for unbelievers. Not only that. I can foresee 'complications' for believers when facing unbelievers over sabbath observance. And that's putting it mildly!

We must be clear as to what we are talking about. If sabbath observance really is a creation ordinance for all men, then all men are obliged to keep the sabbath. Not only that! All the human race must be exposed to all the punishments for sabbath breaking. And not only exposed to them. Those punishments must be meted out on all who break the sabbath. There is no getting round this. This is what sabbath keeping means.

Now, since sabbath observance is such an important matter in Scripture, and the breaking of the sabbath is attended with devastating curses and judgements, we surely need – the pagans, themselves, surely need – the clearest scriptural proof that sabbath observance is a universal and perpetual demand of God for all the human race without exception. As you yourself say:

Disobedience [to the fourth commandment is] treated in Scripture as a grave, moral offence... The death penalty was... required... for this.

---

[10] Murray p169.

There is no offence against God more seriously condemned by the prophets.[11]

Just so! So, on your own argument, sabbath breaking is the most heinous offence; those who break the sabbath (and who does not?) merit the death penalty: 'For its desecration the death penalty was appointed (Ex. 31:14-15). Even the lighting of fires was forbidden (Num. 15:32-36)'.[12]

Then again, you cite 1 John 3:4 (AV): 'Sin is the transgression of the law'.[13] But, as you know, this is a poor, misleading translation. The Greek is: 'Sin is lawlessness', and this is how several versions rightly render it (NKJV, NIV, ESV, NASB, for instance). In fact, the AV is almost unique in its gloss. Sadly, it has caused many to go astray, and think that John was referring to the ten commandments.[14] You do! He was not. The truth is, when a man sins, he breaks some command or another (Rom. 4:15). John was setting out a general principle: to sin is to live in an unprincipled way.[15]

Of course, for Israel in the old covenant, the 'law' in question would have been the Mosaic law above all, yes. And, as you say, he who 'stumbles in one point... has become guilty of all' (Jas. 2:10). I quite agree with the point; namely, if a Jew broke any of the ten commands, he broke the other nine as well. Indeed, if he broke any of the 613 commands of the law, he broke the lot. The law is the law, in its entirety.[16] But, of course, you want to confine this to ten of the commands and, at the same time, broaden it to include the Gentiles, who never had the law.

You also cite 1 John 2:4: 'The one who says: "I have come to know him", and does not keep his commandments, is a liar, and

---

[11] Murray p148.

[12] Murray p147.

[13] Murray p150.

[14] John never once cites the Mosaic law.

[15] There is more that could be said about the translation of 1 John 3:4, but I leave it there.

[16] Take the Passover. Those who broke Passover regulations suffered dire penalties akin to the sabbath (Num. 9:2-3,11-14), yet the Passover was not part of the ten commandments.

the truth is not in him'.[17] While I do not concede that 1 John 2:4 refers to the ten commandments – it clearly refers to Christ's commandments, the law of Christ – nor do I concede that these verses establish that the ten commandments are perpetually binding on all men, let me accept your point for the sake of argument. Since, on your terms, all men ought to know that the sabbath is binding upon them – indeed, all men must know that the sabbath is binding upon them – and we know that to break the commandments is a sin of a very high order, I repeat my request, my demand, for clear and unequivocal evidence that all men do have this working knowledge, both in their conscience and specifically given to them in Scripture.

So as to leave no room for misunderstanding, speaking for myself simply as a man (not, at this point, speaking as a believer), I need proof that I, as a man, must keep the sabbath, and that if I fail to keep it, I face the death sentence. In putting it this way, I am speaking for Mr Everyman. Will you give us that proof?

I must say I am not at all impressed by your argument for universal sabbath-observance based on Exodus 20:10 and Nehemiah 13:16-18: 'In the Old Testament, the observation of the fourth commandment was not required for Jews only, but also for the "sojourner" [alien] who stays with you'.[18] Quite! From this you imply that this proves that sabbath observance is essential for all men without exception. But you surely realise that 'sojourner' speaks of proselytes (or the equivalent at that time) – the word 'proselyte' being an anglicisation of the Septuagint use of the word. Proselytes, the God-fearers, the 'worshippers of God' (Acts 13:43; 16:14; 17:4,17; 18:7), kept the sabbath (and underwent circumcision, and complied with the dietary laws, and so on) as part of their acceptance of Judaism, not because they were obliged to observe such things as creation ordinances binding on all men. Incidentally, why, if all men are obliged to keep the sabbath, did God issue a tautology? Did he need to include the aliens, specifically? Weren't they included already?[19]

---

[17] Murray p160.

[18] Murray p148.

[19] It is Num. 9:14 all over again.

What is involved in being a 'sojourner', a 'stranger', dwelling among the Israelites, is surely set out for us in the regulations for the Passover:

No foreigner is to eat of it. Any slave you have bought may eat of it after you have circumcised him, but a temporary resident and a hired worker may not eat of it... The whole community of Israel must celebrate it. An alien living among you who wants to celebrate the LORD's Passover must have all the males in his household circumcised; then he may take part like one born in the land. No uncircumcised male may eat of it. The same law applies to the native-born and to the alien living among you (Ex. 12:43-49).

In other words, your texts have nothing to say about pagans and the sabbath. They are to do with Jewish adherents, would-be Jews, Jewish converts. You certainly cannot deduce from such passages that *pagans* are obliged to keep the sabbath.

Bearing in mind that by 'the Lord's day' you mean 'the sabbath', you certainly raise the stakes: 'The inability of non-Christians to keep the Lord's day in no way lessens their responsibility to keep it'.[20] Very well. Would you show me the scripture which tells us that unbelievers have a responsibility to keep the Lord's day? Furthermore, would you show me, from Scripture, where all men know they have this responsibility? After all, on your argument it can only mean that when pagans don't keep the sabbath as commanded in Scripture – and who does? – they must be executed. I know that, on your scheme, you feel you can assure believers that they avoid this because Christ has borne the curse for them,[21] but pagans have no such get-out clause, do they? They are not in Christ, they do not have Christ as their curse-bearer, do they? So you must be advocating the death penalty for sabbath breakers, at least for non-Christian sabbath breakers. If so, please spell out who will carry out the inspection, the ground rules for that inspection, the measuring-stick they will use, and who will pronounce and carry out the sentence. Will pagans inflict it on

---

[20] Murray p166.

[21] I know you will say that Christ has removed the curse for believers, leaving the obligation intact, but it will not wash. I refer you to my full argument as set out in my *Christ* pp107-108,404-408; *passim*. You are guilty of special pleading.

fellow-pagans, even on themselves? Or will it fall to believers to do it? And how will believers respond to the exponents of Sharia law when they, in their turn, advocate the execution of those who transgress the Koran?

These are not idle questions. If sabbatarianism is confined within the covers of a book, it is relatively easy to make sweeping claims for it, but what of the practicalities of your proposed jurisprudence – in the real world? As you yourself say: 'For its desecration, the death penalty was appointed (Ex. 31:14-15)'.[22] 'Disobedience [to the fourth commandment is] treated in Scripture as a grave, moral offence... The death penalty was... required... for this. There is no offence against God more seriously condemned by the prophets'.[23] In light of all this, we surely need to have clear answers as to the ground rules I mentioned.

But do you really believe your own teaching? I ask this because you also say: 'It is true that civil law can only restrain public disregard for the Lord's day'.[24] This is manifestly untrue. Civil law can do far more than say that sabbath breaking is wrong: it can make it an offence. It can go further: it can pronounce the death penalty for it, and the officers of the State can carry it out. Why, in our lifetime, the State carried out the death penalty for murder. And in the past, it put to death offenders against several of the laws of Moses, including the ten commandments. It did so for blasphemy and adultery and so on. So why are you so cautious? Why not have the courage of your convictions? Do you want the State to enforce sabbath observance on pain of death? If so, why not say so, straight out?

Of course, you see the inherent illogicality of your case. After all, you talk of the necessity of 'a right understanding of the meaning of the day' if it is not to 'become a dead formality'.[25] Again: 'There can be no delight in Christ's day until his resurrection and redeeming love are known'.[26] And I have already quoted you when you state: 'The inability of non-Christians to

---

[22] Murray p147.
[23] Murray p148.
[24] Murray p168.
[25] Murray p163.
[26] Murray p165.

keep the Lord's day in no way lessens their responsibility'.[27] To cap it all, you admit: 'No one but a Christian can begin a right keeping of the Lord's day. A spiritual day requires a spiritual life'.[28] Moreover, when you say that 'no one but a Christian *can begin a right keeping* of the Lord's day', you are surely admitting the obvious: even *believers* are poor sabbath keepers! The question, therefore, remains: Will a defective observance (bearing in mind James 2:10-11) merit the death penalty? If so, how shall we measure the right degree of attainment? And who will survive? On your own terms, pagans won't! Will any believers?

Nevertheless, despite all these conundrums, you plough on: 'The moral law exists for mankind. Accordingly the Protestant nations professing Christianity buttressed the observation of the first day of the week with civil penalties'.[29] So they did. But they also hanged men for disobeying State/Church laws and refusing to sprinkle their babies, for setting up separatist churches, for refusing to own the King or Queen as Head or Supreme Governor of the Church, and the like. Do you advocate the same today? I ask it because it seems you are still locked into the Westminster Confession with its dreadful love of the magistrate to enforce religion. I notice the verses you cite in support of all these political shenanigans come, unsurprisingly, from the Old Testament.[30] Could we have one or two from the New Testament, please?

In light of all this, bearing in mind the fearful plight in which all mankind find themselves, surely it would be unthinkable that God, the God of infinite love and mercy, would have left us without the clearest testimony that universal sabbath observance is essential, and that the breaking of it is attended with the most severe condemnation. Moreover, we should expect to have this testimony found clearly written, not only in Scripture, but in our consciences by the light of nature, should we not?[31] But is it? Does Joe Bloggs or John Doe know that he must keep the sabbath, and if

---

[27] Murray p166.
[28] Murray p164.
[29] Murray p166.
[30] Murray p167.
[31] Rom. 1:19-21,28,32; 2:12-16.

he fails he faces execution? Has God ever told him that? Does his conscience, the light of nature, tell him?

True, all men are accountable since they know there is a God and that he must be worshipped. In this regard, all men are answerable to God. But this is a far cry from keeping the sabbath. How could any man know *by nature* that God required a weekly sabbath, and that sabbath had to take place sunset to sunset on the last day of each week? How could the Gentiles know that God required them to do no work on that day?[32] Why, the Jews themselves didn't know it until the giving of the manna in Exodus 16! And, of course, in your system, all men today must know *by nature* that, under the new covenant, the day in question, and its hours, have changed. Hmm!

Let me confirm that pagans are not obliged to keep the sabbath. Nehemiah saw some Jews breaking the sabbath, and he also saw pagans bringing 'all kinds of goods' into Jerusalem and selling them to the Jews on the sabbath. He reacted, strongly, to both: he rebuked the Jews for profaning the sabbath, and at the same time he took steps to prevent the pagans from entering the city on that day (Neh. 13:15-22). The episode is highly instructive. Notice how Nehemiah treated the Jews very differently to the pagans. The Jews were breaking God's law which the Lord had given them, whereas Nehemiah merely stopped the pagans from entering the city with their goods. The Jews had to keep the sabbath – God gave it to *them* – but the pagans had to be prevented from interfering with the Jews in *their* observance of the sabbath. What the pagans did with the day *outside* the city was their affair, not Nehemiah's. He was concerned with sabbath observance by the Jews, and only by the Jews. He drove the pagans away when they camped outside the walls – but not for *their* sake. He did it for the sake of the Jews; he wanted the most conducive circumstances possible for *them* to keep the sabbath. The distinction Nehemiah drew between Jews and pagans over sabbath observance could hardly be more clear. Nehemiah was concerned to guard the gates to keep the pagans out. Why? Because he knew the sabbath applied to the Jews and

---

[32] And this was precisely the sin in Neh. 13:15-22.

'the stranger who is within your gates' (Ex. 20:10).[33] As long as they were outside the gates, the pagans were outside his jurisdiction and outside sabbath observance. He was concerned with God's 'wrath on *Israel* by [their] profaning the sabbath' (Neh. 13:18).[34]

Indeed, God could complain that Israel did not keep his laws – which he gave them – but 'have done according to the customs of the Gentiles which are all around you' (Ezek. 11:12); they had 'conformed to the standards of the nations around' them. This makes sense only if God's (and Israel's) laws were different to the laws, principles and standards of the pagans.

Iain, can you not see that this is the point? Before the sabbath episode under Nehemiah, on hearing the law, 'the book of Moses', when it was read to them, the Jews reformed themselves, and separated from the pagans, stopping them from coming into the congregation (Neh. 9:2; 13:1-3). The pagans were not allowed to share in the worship of God or partake of his ordinances, since they had no part in them. The law's remit ran as far as the purity of Israel, and no further. Furthermore, Nehemiah put a stop to the misuse of the temple involving a pagan (Neh. 13:4-9). After this, he dealt with the failure to provide for the levites (Neh. 13:10-14). Then came the issue of the breakdown of the sabbath (Neh. 13:15-22). Once this was sorted out, Nehemiah immediately went on to deal with those Jews who had married pagans (Neh. 13:23-31). But in all this, he rebuked no pagan for being a pagan and acting like a pagan. True, he did address pagans (Neh. 13:21), but as I have pointed out, only to stop them interfering with the Jews on the sabbath. He dealt with Jews, he 'commanded *them*' (Neh. 13:9), he 'warned *them*' (Neh. 13:15), he 'contended with the rulers' of the

---

[33] This is not to be taken literally but metaphorically. It stands for those pagans who converted to Judaism and therefore became virtual Jews, under the authority of Judaism. See my earlier remarks on Ex. 12:43-49.

[34] See my *Christ* pp27-37,337-341, for more on the law being given to Israel and not to all men. See below, where I deal with the fact that the sabbath was a sign of God's covenant with the Jews. The fact that it was such a sign *proves* it must have been a special day for them, for them alone, and not a day for all men. How could it be a sign, a special marker, for Israel, if it belongs to all mankind? See Appendix 2.

Jews, 'the nobles of the *Jews*, and said to *them*' (Neh. 13:11,17), speaking of '*your* fathers... and... *our* God' (Neh. 13:18). As he said: 'Thus I cleansed *them [the Jews]* of everything pagan' (Neh. 13:30). He cleansed the Jews from paganism, and got them back to Jewish (biblical) separation, priesthood support, sabbath and marriage. What was true for the sabbath was equally true for Jewish purity, worship and marriage. The pagans only figured in Nehemiah's reforms because it was their practices and presence which had tainted the Jews and their obedience to God.

Years before, Jeremiah had been a precursor of Nehemiah. He had been told to address 'the kings of Judah, and all Judah, and all the inhabitants of Jerusalem'. The burden of his message was: 'Take heed to yourselves, and bear no burden on the sabbath day... but hallow the sabbath day, as I commanded your fathers' (Jer. 17:19-22). But the Jews refused, even though God promised them that if they kept the sabbath, then Jerusalem and its surrounding cities, the kings, princes and men of Judah would be blessed in their sacrifices to the Lord, and, on the other hand, warned them that if they continued to refuse, and profaned the sabbath, then Jerusalem would be destroyed (Jer. 17:23-27).

Isaiah said much the same thing:

If you turn away your foot from the sabbath, from doing your pleasure on my holy day, and call the sabbath a delight, the holy day of the LORD honourable, and shall honour him, not doing your own ways, nor finding your own pleasure, nor speaking your own words, then you shall delight yourself in the LORD; and I will cause you to ride on the high hills of the earth, and feed you with the heritage of Jacob your father. The mouth of the LORD has spoken (Isa. 58:13-14).

The point is clear. The sabbath was Jewish. If the Jews kept the day, their economy and religion would flourish; if they profaned the day, their system would be blighted. Where did God ever say such things to Gentiles?

So how can you allege that all men are obliged to keep the sabbath? Nehemiah did not tell the pagans as much. If it had been the duty of the Gentiles to keep the sabbath, not only would Nehemiah have reminded them of it, but God himself must have commanded them to keep it – indeed, you think he commanded all men so at creation – and he must have told them precisely how they should keep it. Otherwise, it could not have been their duty to observe the day. They could not be blamed for not doing what they had never been told to do. How could they be accountable if they had received no law on the subject? No law? No sin! For 'sin is not imputed when there is no law' (Rom. 5:13). I ask again: When did God command the Gentiles to keep the sabbath, and tell them how to keep it? When did God give precise instructions to the Gentiles regarding the sabbath?

The answer is, of course, never. Nehemiah did not rebuke the pagans for breaking sabbath laws. The reason is obvious: the sabbath did not apply to them. And this is not an isolated case. In all the countless passages where the prophets condemned the nations (in Isaiah, Jeremiah, Ezekiel, Amos and so on), there is never a hint that God through the prophets ever complained that pagans broke the sabbath. Never a hint! Are we to deduce they all kept it? Or that it did not apply to them? Which is it? God rebuked the Jews when they broke the sabbath. Take Amos who, when he condemned Judah in the name of the Lord, told them why God had punished them; it was 'because they have despised the law of the LORD, and have not kept his commandments' (Amos 2:4); and as for Israel, he specifically referred to sabbath offences (Amos 8:2,5). In contrast, when addressing any other nation, Amos did not mention God's law.

And when we come to the New Testament and read the list of Gentile sins in Romans 1:18-32, sabbath breaking is conspicuous by its absence. Once again, does this signify that the Gentiles of the time were not sabbath breakers? If so, it can only mean either they exceeded the Jews in keeping the sabbath – and of this there is no evidence whatsoever – or else they never were given nor were expected to keep the sabbath. Which is it? And what of Galatians 5:19? 'The acts of the flesh are obvious: sexual immorality, impurity and debauchery; idolatry and witchcraft; hatred, discord, jealousy, fits of rage, selfish ambition, dissensions, factions and envy; drunkenness, orgies, and the like. I warn you, as I did before, that those who live like this will not inherit the kingdom of God'. Once again there is no mention of sabbath breaking. How can you account for this? If the sabbath is a perpetual and universal requirement – that is, a duty for all men in all ages – and since the punishment for disobedience is so severe, why is sabbath breaking missing in this list of 'the acts of the flesh'?

Finally in this section, I return to your remarks on what you call the 'complications' in sabbath observance for believers.[35] Have you given any thought to the 'complications' that *pagans* might have in carrying out a universal demand for sabbath observance? You are also concerned to make the sabbath 'bright and happy' for children and young people in the families of believers.[36] Where do we get instruction about this in Scripture? We get it in the Reformed and evangelical manuals of piety, yes, but please show me a biblical example of it. As before, have you given any thought as to how pagans might make the sabbath 'bright' for their children? Would you show me a biblical example of a Gentile – that is, a non-Jew (or one who is not a Jewish proselyte) – keeping the sabbath, let alone making it 'bright' for their children? How should they make it bright for *themselves*? And, of course, while it is true that many do thank God for parents who gave them a Christian sabbath,[37] what about those who testify to being put off by the experience?

Yet again, though you approve of J.C.Ryle who 'knew very well that Sunday laws make no one Christian, but they did something to keep the day special and to encourage church going. Many were brought to hear the Bible, and public respect for God spread though national life to a degree scarcely conceivable today',[38] I would like you to take a look at the other side of that coin. Christendom has been responsible for some of the most dreadful curses ever inflicted upon the church (and the world). One of these is to turn the church into a kind of fishing lake in which to gather unbelievers so that they can be evangelised. This notion is utterly foreign to the new covenant. It has also produced a horde of nominal but unregenerate Christendom-Christians, men and women who are eternally deceived.

Sabbatarianism may have produced 'quiet Sundays', which believers of 'a certain age' look back upon with nostalgia, but I

---

[35] Murray p169.
[36] Murray p169.
[37] Murray p169.
[38] Murray p168.

wonder how many pagans in those days became bitter towards the gospel because the State enforced the wishes of believers (the minority) upon their unwilling fellows. Ryle's enforced sabbatarianism certainly might have funnelled unbelievers into church in his day – many had nowhere else to go which was free, dry and warm when everything else had been shut up by law – and it might have led to the conversion of some, but how many were deluded into thinking they were believers, when they were not, and others effectually hardened against believers, and hence against Christ and his gospel?

Bringing this up to date: I have been preaching for over 50 years, almost always in separatist churches (which are supposed to demand a regenerate membership). Even so, most of the churches where I have preached have been plagued by attenders (for decades) who are unregenerate, and utterly hardened to the gospel. I suggest that if an enforced sabbatarianism (enforced by whatever means thought necessary) were to be coupled with the growing emphasis on friendship evangelism – which we see all too evidently about us – we will have brewed a toxic mixture which will lead to the delusion and damnation of countless men and women.

In short, your idea of an enforced sabbatarianism is not only unbiblical; it is unworkable. Moreover, it is a sharp double-edged weapon, one which is liable to cut the one who uses it, to say nothing of the spiritual damage it might inflict on millions of miserable pagans who suffer under it. That damage might well be eternal.

I close this section with Paul's words:

Though we live in the world, we do not wage war as the world does. The weapons we fight with are not the weapons of the world. On the contrary, they have divine power to demolish strongholds. We demolish arguments and every pretension that sets itself up against the knowledge of God, and we take captive every thought to make it obedient to Christ (2 Cor. 10:3-5).

The world, not least the Moslem world, might well use politics and the sword to advance Islam or whatever, but in order to advance the gospel, believers forego every weapon that is forged in any foundry outside the new covenant. In particular, believers should

31

not adopt your jurisprudence, drawn, as it is, entirely from the Mosaic law and the old covenant.

The sabbath in Genesis

Clearly, Genesis 2:3 is your leading text. Indeed, *everything* hangs upon it. First, you make it your epigraph.[39] Then again, you expressly say that this verse is crucial in this debate. And as you conclude your positive answer to the question: 'Is Genesis 2:3 for us?', you state:

This is a discussion of no minor significance. As I have said, a great deal depends on which conclusion [yes or no] is right and which wrong. If the appointment of the day of rest comes from the time of creation, then the words of the Lord: 'The sabbath was made for man' (Mark 2:27) refer to all mankind, and the fourth commandment has divine authority today. If the appointment belongs to the time of Israel[40] then it has no universal significance, and the fourth commandment is only for the Jews.[41]

I could not agree more.[42] *The sabbath was only for the Jews unless it can be proved that it was given to Adam, and hence to all mankind.* You say it can be proved. I say it cannot. Since the consequences are so far-reaching, and far-reaching for so many people, you will understand that it is essential for us to have the clearest of proofs that Genesis 2:3 *does* apply to us; that is, in Genesis 2:3 the sabbath *was* given to all men and for all time. I submit that you do not give us that clear proof.

The truth is, you fail because it is not possible to prove it. The sabbath was not a creation ordinance. It was not given to all men in Adam. It was not even given to the patriarchs.[43] It was given to the

---

[39] Murray p139.

[40] That is, in the wilderness just before, and leading to, the giving of the law to Israel at Sinai (Exodus 16 & 20).

[41] Murray p147.

[42] Apart from your use of 'is'. The sabbath *was* for the Jews as long as the old covenant was in place.

[43] Compare John 7:22. Circumcision was given to Abraham and was later incorporated in the Mosaic economy. Christ made it very clear that the original giving of circumcision was to 'the fathers', not to Moses. Where is the corresponding passage for what is supposed to have happened for

Jews through Moses (Ex. 31:12-17; Neh. 9:14; Ezek. 20:12). It was a central part of God's covenant with Israel, his special people (Deut. 4:1-8,44-45; 5:1-3; 29:1,10-15,25,29).[44] It lasted as long as the law, the old covenant – which was until the coming of Christ (Gal. 3:19). It was not ordained for the human race.

But what about: 'The sabbath was made for man' (Mark 2:27)? Christ does not mean that all men, in all ages, are required to keep the sabbath – which is what you believe.[45] Christ is telling the Pharisees that man is more important than the sabbath. After all, even on your reckoning, man was created before the sabbath. The truth is, of course, the sabbath was given to Israel in the wilderness when the sabbath was given to man (that is, the Jew); man (the Jew) was not created for the sabbath.[46]

Let me look, therefore, at your claim that Genesis 2:3 proves that the sabbath applies to all men, because God, in that verse, was commanding Adam – and, through him, all men – to observe the sabbath.[47] I deny this.

Nevertheless, if we grant, for the sake of argument, that you are right, and God did command Adam to keep the sabbath, he was in effect, giving him the fourth commandment. More, he must have been giving him all ten (and more). After all, we know that the ten commandments stand or fall together (Jas. 2:10-11).[48] I say your case depends upon Adam having the ten commandments.

I admit that you nowhere state that God gave Adam the ten commandments – although, as you know, many Reformed teachers are not shy at asserting this. But if Adam was given a

---

the sabbath (namely, that God gave the day to Adam, and restated it to Moses)?

[44] The words 'him who is not here with us today' (Deut. 29:14-15) refer to the descendants of the children of Israel, not to all the rest of the human race.

[45] Murray p147.

[46] Calvin on the verse: 'Is not this a foolish attempt to overturn the purpose of God, when they demand to the injury of men that observation of the sabbath which he intended to be advantageous?'

[47] Murray pp141-147.

[48] You certainly think so: 'There is a unity to the moral law [in your terms, the ten commandments]. Like a sheet of glass, if broken at one point, the whole is shattered' (Murray p150).

commandment to observe the sabbath, as you claim he was, what else could it be, other than the fourth of the ten? Indeed, some of the arguments you use to support your claim can only mean that Adam *was* given the fourth commandment.[49]

Adam, therefore, must have been given the law against sabbath breaking (and, with it, the law against idolatry, blasphemy, adultery, lying, theft, and so on). And he must have been given all this *before* he had sinned.[50] Really? At a time when he had no concept of sin, no idea what theft was, had no opportunity to commit adultery, let alone any concept of it, even before he had a wife (see below), yet God gave him the law on these and many other matters, and did so for his immediate and continued obedience, with all the warnings and punishments for disobedience. And all before he fell! Really?

Do you question this? Do you deny that if Adam was given the fourth commandment, he was told the consequences of breaking it? If so, may I suggest you compare God's command to Adam not to eat the fruit of the tree of the knowledge of good and evil: God spelled out the consequences of disobedience, and did so explicitly:

The LORD God commanded the man: 'You are free to eat from any tree in the garden; but you must not eat from the tree of the knowledge of good and evil, for when you eat of it you will surely die' (Gen. 2:16-17).

Do not miss the: 'You must not eat from the tree... *for* when you eat of it you will surely die'.[51] Similarly for the sabbath, *if* God had commanded Adam to keep the sabbath, Adam must have had the punishment for sabbath breaking made clear to him – before he fell. And so for all the other commands. Where do we read this? Can you not see how ridiculous the notion is?

---

[49] In order to maintain the pace of what now follows, I set out my case in Appendix 1. To get the full force of my argument, that excursus should be read at this point.

[50] In addition, he must also have been given all the other 600 or more laws which constituted 'the law'. The Bible knows nothing of the Reformed (and Medieval) tripartite division of the law.

[51] When God commands, he spells out the consequences of disobedience. Take just two examples: Josh. 24:14-27; John 3:16-21,36.

I am sure you can! For you partly bite this bullet, although you try to limit the damage by restricting your argument to one of the ten commands; the sabbath. This is not possible! But even allowing it to be the case, the problem remains. Did Adam have the fourth commandment? If so, what did he make of the servants and the alien mentioned in that commandment? Who were they? We could widen the debate: When he was given the tenth commandment, whatever did he make about coveting his neighbour's wife? What was 'coveting', who was his 'neighbour', and who was his 'neighbour's wife'? Indeed, who or what was a 'wife'?[52]

So how do you handle this conundrum? In this way: 'That God sanctified one day in seven for unfallen man is enough for us to know, without asking why it could be so'.[53] Hmm! Are you really happy with this? Does it satisfy you? It fails to satisfy me, I'm afraid.

Let me explain, by way of three comments. *First*, your statement, of course, if it is right, means that you now have hit upon a sovereign argument for buttressing your case in every particular, an effective get-out clause against every objection. It establishes every claim, and answers every possible objection, killing every objection stone dead. As a consequence, it would seem that your attempted justification of the case is quite unnecessary – besides being inadequate. But is the basic argument strong enough to bear the massive weight you heap upon it? And, as I will show, your claims are massive and far-reaching. This ploy would seem to answer all the claims that you make for the sabbath

---

[52] See below.

[53] Murray p143. Incidentally, by your use of 'unfallen', I detect that you do think Adam was given the fourth commandment. Yet we know that 'the law... was added *because of transgressions* until the Seed [Christ] to whom the promise referred had come' (Gal. 3:19). Men were sinners before the giving of the law, of course, but the law turned sin into transgression – where there is no law, there is no transgression (Rom. 4:15; 5:13). What is more, while the entrance of the law did not create sin, it promoted it, increased it, exhibited it, defined it. This is what the law does. This is why it was 'added'. It exposes sin, and convicts the offender of it (Rom. 3:19-20; 7:7-13). It arouses sin (Rom. 7:5,7-11), brings a curse (Gal. 3:10), slavery (Gal. 4:1-8) and wrath (Rom. 4:15). See my *Christ* p131.

in Genesis, and, therefore, for the entire debate, and all without further ado. All you have to do is make the assertion: 'The Bible tells us that all men in Adam were given the sabbath, and although this gives us insuperable problems and leads us into all sorts of contradictions, we simply have to accept it'. Of course, if the Bible really does say it, you are perfectly correct.[54] But does the Bible say it? That is the question. And if it does, you should prove it.

Secondly, I notice your ubiquitous gloss in this section (and throughout your work) of 'one day in seven' – a heavily loaded phrase in this context: 'God sanctified one day in seven'. He never did! He sanctified the seventh day. I will return to this.

Thirdly, can you not see that you are arguing in a circle? or, to put it another way, begging the question? You claim – you assume – that Adam was given the law. You run into difficulties. You then say that we have to live with these difficulties since we know that Adam was given the law. Hey presto, back to the beginning! And this is not the last time you use this technique.

Nor does this signal the end to the weakness of your argument on this vital point about Genesis. Take this: 'The division of time into a seven-day week *is best understood* as originating at the creation and in connection with Genesis 2:3. Those who believe...'.[55] This may be right. But, even if it is, it offers no proof for what is unprovable; namely, that the patriarchs kept the sabbath. We know they worshipped, sacrificed and built altars, married, worked – we have abundant testimony of it. Why no corresponding testimony about their keeping the sabbath? Especially since, on your argument, it is the pinnacle of creation.[56]

In short, the evidence you produce to support your claim that Genesis 2:3 speaks of God's command to Adam regarding the sabbath, and hence the universal and perpetual observance of the sabbath by all men, is often flimsy in the extreme; in truth, it smacks of a 'clutching at straws'. It cannot be anything else, of course, since after all there is no *scriptural* support for the claim,

---

[54] See my *The Gospel Offer is Free*, Brachus, Biggleswade, first edition 2004, second edition 2012, for the seeming contradiction between God's decree and his desire to see sinners saved.

[55] Murray p143, emphasis mine.

[56] Murray pp140-141.

as I will prove, and as has been admitted by many of your fellow-sabbatarians.

The truth is, by taking Genesis 2:3 in the way that you do, you lessen the import of the text. As you say,[57] God's seventh-day rest was the climax of creation. I agree. What is more, this is of the utmost importance. God sanctified the seventh day, the final day of the week, resting from his work of creation. That is, he separated it, marked it out with a purpose in mind – a purpose which involved man, certainly – but a purpose which would only come to fruition at the proper time.[58] What purpose? If you are right, then the climax of God's creation was that Adam (and, therefore, all men) should enjoy rest on the seventh day of each week. This is creation's *climax*? Really? This cannot be right. It takes far too low a view of God's goal in creation. The climax of creation, God's intention in creating the universe, was incomparably higher than a rest day for the human race. The 'rest' in question is very much more than a weekly rest for man.

As with creation, so with every work of God, the ultimate end was God and his glory: 'For of him and through him and to him are all things, to whom be glory for ever' (Rom. 11:36; see also Rev. 4:11). In particular, Christ is the beginning and the end of everything. Everything! He is 'the alpha and the omega, the first and the last, the beginning and the end' (Rev. 1:8,11; 21:6; 22:13). 'Christ is all, and is in all' (Col. 3:11). 'By him all things were created that are in heaven and that are on earth... All things were created through him and for him... that in all things he might have the pre-eminence' (Col. 1:16-18).

Let me underline this: all things – including the seventh-day rest of creation – all things were created *for* Christ – *for Christ, not man* – that in all things – in *all* things, including the seventh-day rest – Christ might have the pre-eminence. Creation did not reach a climax with something merely *for man*; certainly it was not a weekly day of rest for him during his earthly pilgrimage. Creation's end, its climax, was Christ; it was for him, for his

---

[57] Murray pp140-141.

[58] Compare Gal. 1:15, which refers to God's electing, separating decree concerning Saul, a decree to be fulfilled in due time. Compare also Rom. 8:29-30.

praise, for his glory. And in that, of course, the ultimate and eternal glory of God:

God also has highly exalted [Christ] and given him the name which is above every name, that at the name of Jesus every knee should bow, of those in heaven, and of those on earth, and of those under the earth, and that every tongue should confess that Jesus Christ is Lord, to the glory of God the Father (Phil. 2:9-11).

Then comes the end, when [Christ] delivers the kingdom to God the Father, when he puts an end to all rule and all authority and power. For he must reign till he has put all enemies under his feet... Now when all things are made subject to him, then the Son himself will also be subject to him who put all things under him, that God may be all in all (1 Cor. 15:24-28; see also John 3:14; 5:19-27; 8:28; 12:28,32-34; 1 Cor. 3:21-23; Heb. 2:5-9).

In particular, as these extracts show, it was salvation in and through the work of Christ – surely God's greatest accomplishment – that was and is the real sabbath. This was the real climax of creation. And, it goes without saying, it was in God's mind right at the start. Notice how the Genesis record of the seventh day does not have the usual 'evening and morning' attached to it; there was an in-built sense of eternity even at the beginning. God's blessing of the seventh day was not concerned with a weekly one-seventh proportion of man's experience of the revolving 168 hours, (as you are, with your 'one day in seven').

God had in mind the ultimate rest – rest in Christ. Christ is the climax of creation; his glory, and the believer's eternal rest in him is the true sabbath (Heb. 4:9-11).[59] All the other 'rests' were pointing to this (Heb. 3:7 – 4:11); in particular, God's rest on the seventh day after creation augured this great eternal sabbath in Christ.

And of course this is true, not only of that original seventh day, but of the weekly sabbath for Israel in the Mosaic covenant – which is not in Genesis 2, of course. How could it be? Israel did not exist at that time, nor did Moses or his law! Indeed, are we not told explicitly that the law was introduced 430 years *after* Abraham (Gal. 3:17)? And yet you want us to believe that it was

---

[59] Many people see only a day of the week in Heb. 4:9-11; it is a travesty. I will come back to this.

given to Adam hundreds of years *before* Abraham! As I have already noted, are we not told that the law was added *because* of transgression (Gal. 3:19)? Yet you want us to believe that the law was given to Adam *before* he had sinned!

No! The sabbath was given to *Israel*, given to Israel through Moses in the wilderness, and later ratified on Sinai. Moreover, it symbolised spiritual rest for the believer in Christ now, in the new covenant, leading to his eternal rest in him (Heb. 4:3-10). As did all the rest of the old covenant.

It is this that puts the seventh day in its proper setting, far beyond a mere weekly rest for man.[60]

The upshot is, the sabbath was not a creation *ordinance*. This is borne out by the fact that in the entire book of Genesis there is not a single command to any man to keep the sabbath, there is no example of any man keeping the sabbath, and there is no condemnation of any man for breaking the sabbath. In short, the sabbath – as far as a weekly observance for man is concerned – is completely unknown in Genesis.

God rested on the seventh day, but there is no record in the creation account that he commanded man to observe it. Genesis 2:1-3 is a statement of what God *did*, not Adam's *duty* – of God's action, not his command. It was God's rest, not man's. This is to state the obvious. But, sadly, the obvious needs to be stated! Indeed, it seems to me that the passage is a revelation of this to Moses when he wrote the book, not a record of God's revelation to Adam. That is to say, is there any proof that Adam even knew that God rested on the seventh day, let alone that God commanded him to keep it? There is no evidence whatsoever to justify the claim that God revealed to Adam that he rested or that he commanded Adam to keep the day. While I do not take the line you rightly argue against – that it was Moses who 'inserted' 'the words of

---

[60] If this might be thought somewhat strained, compare Gen. 1:1 – 2:3 with John 1:1-5. I owe this thought to Walter Senenko. Another friend drew my attention to the principle in 1 Cor. 15:46: 'The spiritual did not come first, but the natural, and after that the spiritual'. In this case, the weekly sabbath pictured the spiritual sabbath, leading to the eternal sabbath. I will return to the old (Testament and covenant) being the shadow of the substance of the new.

Genesis 2:3'[61] – there is no *biblical* evidence that Adam knew that God rested.

What is more, you should take full cognisance of Genesis 2:20-24. Adam knew that he was given Eve, and that she had come from his bone; he said so. But when the scripture goes on to assert: 'For this reason a man will leave his father and mother and be united to his wife, and they will become one flesh' (Gen. 2:24), this strikes me as a later (Mosaic) explanation – an explanation, not an insertion. What concept, in the day the woman was formed, would Adam and Eve have of 'father' and 'mother'? Of course, 'the man and his wife were both naked, and they felt no shame' (Gen. 2:25) could be Adamic, yes, but even this may be a Mosaic comment. I think it very likely.

And what about Noah and the flood? Noah had to take animals, both clean and unclean, into the ark (Gen. 7:2,8; 8:20). But what is this 'clean' and 'unclean'? Where is that defined? In the law in the book of Leviticus, and beyond. In other words, Moses, with hindsight, is explaining, offering a comment on Noah's obedience and action.

All I am saying is, we must not forget that Adam, Noah and the other patriarchs did not have the book of Genesis to read. And this has ramifications for us. The truth is, we must not read Christendom and covenant theology back into the Bible. How often this is done! With respect, it is what you are doing. What are we told in Scripture? God rested, God sanctified and blessed the seventh day, yes. But did he command man to keep it? Does it say so? No! And as for accuracy, please note that the English word *sabbath* does not appear in the creation record; as a matter of fact, it does not appear in the whole of Genesis. These matters must not be dismissed as trivial, or glossed over.

Let me close this section by returning to the way I started it. You and I are agreed that the sabbath was only for the Jews unless it can be proved that it was given to Adam. I stand by that. I am sure you do. But do you think you have proved the sabbath was given to Adam? I don't! That the sabbath is for all men, therefore,

---

[61] Murray p146.

you have signally failed to prove. As Scripture makes plain, the sabbath was for the Jew in the old covenant, and only for the Jew.

Change of day

I agree with you when you say:

The key question is this: If there was a transfer of spiritual significance from the seventh day to the first, who authorised the change?[62]

You are convinced that in the new covenant the sabbath is still in force, but the day has changed from the seventh to the first: 'For Christians the special day had become the first day of the week'.[63] (You also assume, but do not seek to justify or even mention it, that the way of measuring the day has changed from Jewish timekeeping – sunset to sunset – to Roman – midnight to midnight). How and when was this major change put into effect, and by whose authority? I will look at what you say on this a little more under the next heading; I simply raise the question here. Did Christ, himself, directly change the sabbath? Were the apostles responsible for it? Or who or what did it? If the sabbath has been changed so radically – not only the day of the week and the timing of the day, but by a massive change in the purpose of the day[64] –

---

[62] Murray p155.

[63] Murray pp154-155; see also p156; *passim*.

[64] The sabbath was a day of rest. The Jews had to cease (that is the meaning of 'sabbath' as you yourself say – Murray p140) from work (see Ex. 16:14-36; 20:8-11; 34:21; 35:2-3; Lev. 23:3; Deut. 5:12-15; Neh. 10:31; 13:15-22; Jer. 17:21-27). That is what God commanded. The sabbath was not primarily a day of worship, but a day of rest. The pattern of weekly worship did not exist in the Old Testament law. The synagogue introduced it in the inter-testamental period. Even then, rest and sabbath were synonymous. While still under the old covenant, resting is precisely what the women did on the day after Christ was crucified: 'And they rested on the sabbath according to the commandment' (Luke 23:56). It is not said that they worshipped. As for Isa. 66:22-24; Ezek. 46:1-12; Zech. 14:16-21, I read all such as old-covenant prophecies of the new covenant. Pre-millennialists will probably expect them to be literally fulfilled in the millennium. I don't. But neither view has any bearing on Jewish

41

and since the sabbath is the fourth commandment in the unchangeable law of God, do you not think we ought to have some clear scriptural statement to put this change beyond doubt? Why do you not give us this clear biblical statement? Has there been any other commandment of the unchangeable law of God that has been so altered, yet so-say keeping the command intact? And why is this the only old-covenant shadow to come over into the new covenant? We don't circumcise, sacrifice, go to the temple, use a priest, have an altar, do we? In all such matters, we dwell on the spiritual fulfilment in Christ, and have nothing to do with the external shadow. So why not the sabbath? Why is the sabbath unique? On what grounds is it unique? Who authorised all this?

Seeing Scripture never speaks of a change of the day or its use, there is really nothing more to say. All talk of a change of day is little more than speculation based on wished-for inference. In any case, since we are talking about the *unchangeable* law of God...

Sleight of hand

I am not trying to be offensive, but I can think of no other way of putting it; perhaps 'conjuring trick', 'begging the question', 'arguing in a circle', or 'glosses' might fit the bill. What am I talking about? I draw your attention to your use of phrases such as 'one day in seven', 'every seventh day', or the equivalent;[65] the way you equate 'the law' and 'the ten commandments';[66] the way you repeatedly move from 'sabbath' to 'Lord's day';[67] loaded, misleading (not to say, bordering on erroneous) statements such as: 'The Jews were given a "fuller" revelation of the sabbath at Sinai';[68] 'The sabbath was also at this time[69] related to God's

---

observance of the sabbath in the old covenant. The sabbath was not designed to be a day of worship.

[65] Murray pp141,143,152,156.

[66] Murray pp158,160; *passim*.

[67] Murray p143; *passim*.

[68] Murray p147. Since the sabbath was given to Israel in Ex. 16, it could be said that Sinai was a 'fuller' revelation. But you did not mean *that*.

[69] Which? Just before you were speaking of 'the time of Moses' and the time of Nehemiah. You go on to cite Exodus, Numbers, Deuteronomy and Ezekiel.

redemptive purposes. It was now a memorial not only of creation but of the nation's deliverance from Egypt (Deut. 5:15). The special day became a covenant sign of God's saving work in their midst (Ex. 31:16; Ezek. 20:12)';[70] your constant assumption of the supposed threefold division of the law into moral, ceremonial (and judicial);[71] your talk of 'the ceremonial law' as though it were a scriptural phrase;[72] your repeated assumption of, and references to, 'man's continued obligation' to keep the sabbath;[73] your claim that the sabbath was a time of public worship;[74] and so on. Then again, since you use 'sabbath' and 'Lord's day' as interchangeable throughout your work, you frequently talk of the Lord's day as 'the day of rest'.[75]

All such glosses, conjuring tricks and sleight of hand, are fundamental to the Reformed case, judging by their ubiquitous use in their works on the sabbath. Would you establish all these points from Scripture, please?

Are you sure the headings over (or under)[76] the psalms are inspired? You seem to think so.[77] Would you prove it, please? Are you sure that 'the day' spoken of in Psalm 118 is the sabbath? The texts you cite (Matt. 21:42; Acts 4:11) signally fail to establish it for me, I'm afraid.[78]

---

[70] Murray p147. This is loaded. The day did not 'become' 'a' covenant sign of spiritual redemption or salvation. Under the *old* covenant, God *gave* it to Israel as *the* sign that they were distinct from all other nations. I think I can detect your covenant theology with its different administrations of the one covenant of grace. This is wrong. The two covenants are not one and the same. The sabbath was a vital part of the old covenant, which covenant was very different indeed to the new covenant. I will return to this extract.

[71] Murray pp147-153; *passim.*

[72] Murray p153. The threefold division of the law is quite wrong. See my *Christ* pp100-104,392-400.

[73] Murray pp149,160-169.

[74] Murray pp142-143,150-152; *passim.* See the earlier note on the inter-testamental change from 'rest' to 'rest and worship'.

[75] Murray pp143-152, for instance.

[76] Some teachers think the headings refer to the preceding psalm, not the following.

[77] Murray p149.

[78] Murray p158.

As for begging the question, or arguing in a circle, how about this? You quote Matthew 28:20 and Mark 2:28, and then go on to say: 'In the light of such words it is unthinkable that men changed the seventh day to the first without the authority of the one to whom that day belongs'.[79] Quite! Having assumed the apostles did change the sabbath to the first day of the week, you then argue that since they did change it they must have had the Lord's authority for doing it! *QED.* It really won't do, you know. We deserve better than this!

Then again, you speak of 'the principle of one day in seven kept specially for God, as taught in the fourth commandment, and beginning with the Genesis pattern'.[80] Please tell me what version of the Bible you are using. All the versions I use say that God sanctified the *seventh* day, and commanded Israel to keep the seventh day, sunset to sunset – *not* 'one day in seven'. What would you say if men pulled this trick on other commands? It strikes me you are doing much the same as the Pharisees did with their talk of Corban and the like (Mark 7:11). If so, you must surely come under Christ's condemnation. Why not stick to your own rubric: 'The law... was not open for any man-made additions or alterations'?[81] I quite agree. No 'additions or alterations' ought ever to be attempted. Not even of the Reformed variety.

And what about this for sloppy exegesis? I cannot believe that you think Romans 2:15 teaches that the law 'has authority over Gentile as well as Jew'.[82] Just to read the verse in its context makes it clear as noonday that while Gentiles have a rudimentary knowledge of right and wrong in the conscience, they certainly do *not* have the law:

All who sin apart from the law will also perish apart from the law, and all who sin under the law will be judged by the law. For it is not those who hear the law who are righteous in God's sight, but it is those who obey the law who will be declared righteous. (Indeed, when Gentiles, who do not have the law, do by nature things required by the law, they are a law for themselves, even though they do not have the law, since

---

[79] Murray p156.
[80] Murray p156.
[81] Murray p156.
[82] Murray p149.

they show that the requirements of the law are written on their hearts, their consciences also bearing witness, and their thoughts now accusing, now even defending them). This will take place on the day when God will judge men's secrets through Jesus Christ, as my gospel declares (Rom. 2:12-16).[83]

And where do you get this: 'Children at Ephesus were to be taught the commandments (Eph. 6:2)'?[84] When writing to the believers at Ephesus, Paul certainly uses the fifth commandment as an illustration, I agree, and I am quite prepared to accept that believing parents would refer to the law, the whole law,[85] as part of all Scripture, when instructing their children (2 Tim. 3:14-17). But that children at Ephesus – including children of pagans – were to be *instructed* in the law, (and, presumably, told they were under it for sanctification)? Taught by whom? I guess you will say that you confine your remarks to the children of believers, but if you do, may I put a question to you? Since you think that all men, women and children are duty-bound, both by reason of creation and being under the law[86] (in your terms, the ten commandments), to keep the sabbath, on what grounds do you limit your prescription to children of believers? Shouldn't all children be taught the commandments?

There is another point. If the church must teach children the commandments, how does this square with Paul's: 'Woe to me if I do not preach the gospel!' (1 Cor. 9:16)? And we know what he meant by that:

I resolved to know nothing while I was with you except Jesus Christ and him crucified (1 Cor. 2:2).
We... preach... Jesus Christ as Lord (2 Cor. 4:5).

---

[83] For more on Rom. 2:14-15, see my *Christ* pp38-48,342-347.
[84] Murray p149.
[85] As Paul did himself. He occasionally treats it as a paradigm (Rom. 13:8-10; Gal. 5:14-15; Eph. 6:1-4), and he also refers to parts of it outside the ten commandments by way of illustration (1 Cor. 5:6-8; 9:7-14, and so on). Even so, he is willing to use anything to make his point, including the history of Israel (1 Cor. 10:1-11; see also Rom. 4:23-24; 15:4), nature, common sense or Greek poets (Acts 17:28-29; 1 Cor. 11:14; Tit. 1:12-13).
[86] Murray p157.

Is there any biblical example of an apostle teaching believers – let alone their children – the commandments?

Then again, with respect, your interpretation of Romans 6:14 leaves a great deal to be desired. You say, quite rightly: 'This text is often misunderstood'. Yes, this text is often misunderstood – not least by Reformed theologians! I am afraid you are a case in point, for you water down the apostle's words by speaking in terms of condemnation.[87] If you read the context (from Romans 6:11 – 7:6), you will see quite clearly that the believer has died to the law, lock stock and barrel, not simply to its condemnation. The apostle's two illustrations of slavery and marriage make the point. Let me quote the passage in full for you. I make no apology for this. Sabbatarians are too fond of proof texts.[88] Let us have passages! Here is a mighty passage of Scripture:

Count yourselves dead to sin but alive to God in Christ Jesus. Therefore do not let sin reign in your mortal body so that you obey its evil desires. Do not offer the parts of your body to sin, as instruments of wickedness, but rather offer yourselves to God, as those who have been brought from death to life; and offer the parts of your body to him as instruments of righteousness. For sin shall not be your master, because you are not under law, but under grace.
What then? Shall we sin because we are not under law but under grace? By no means! Don't you know that when you offer yourselves to someone to obey him as slaves, you are slaves to the one whom you obey – whether you are slaves to sin, which leads to death, or to obedience, which leads to righteousness? But thanks be to God that, though you used to be slaves to sin, you wholeheartedly obeyed the form of teaching to which you were entrusted. You have been set free from sin and have become slaves to righteousness. I put this in human terms because you are weak in your natural selves. Just as you used to offer the parts of your body in slavery to impurity and to ever-increasing wickedness, so now offer them in slavery to righteousness leading to holiness. When you were slaves to sin, you were free from the control of righteousness. What benefit did you reap at that time from the things you are now ashamed of ? Those things result in death! But now that you have been set free from sin and have become slaves to God, the benefit you reap leads to holiness, and the result is

---

[87] Murray p157.

[88] It's like building a pyramid by making it stand on its point. Let's have the base well fixed first. I owe this way of putting it to David White.

eternal life. For the wages of sin is death, but the gift of God is eternal life in Christ Jesus our Lord.

Do you not know, brothers – for I am speaking to men who know the law – that the law has authority over a man only as long as he lives? For example, by law a married woman is bound to her husband as long as he is alive, but if her husband dies, she is released from the law of marriage. So then, if she marries another man while her husband is still alive, she is called an adulteress. But if her husband dies, she is released from that law and is not an adulteress, even though she marries another man. So, my brothers, you also died to the law through the body of Christ, that you might belong to another, to him who was raised from the dead, in order that we might bear fruit to God. For when we were controlled by the flesh, the sinful passions aroused by the law were at work in our bodies, so that we bore fruit for death. But now, by dying to what once bound us, we have been released from the law so that we serve in the new way of the Spirit, and not in the old way of the written code (Rom. 6:11 – 7:6).

The fact is, the believer has been translated out of the realm of law – letter – and into the realm of the Spirit, having died to the law.[89] This is the glorious teaching of Romans 6:14 – 8:4. I am afraid your conception of all this misses the apostle's point by a long chalk. If you read Romans 7:4-6 and 2 Corinthians 3 aloud – Paul's setting out of the believer's glorious condition under the ministry of the Spirit – and compare that with your letter-ridden interpretation of such passages, the difference will be patent. You end up trying to apply to the believer the very law – the killing, condemning law – to which he has died in Christ (Rom. 7:4-6; 8:2; 2 Cor. 3:6-9; Gal. 2:19; 5:18).[90]

Just a few more examples of the sort of things covered by 'sleight of hand'.

In your paragraph starting with: 'The inability of non-Christians to keep the Lord's day...', you quote: 'By the law is the knowledge of sin' (Rom. 3:20; 7:7).[91] I know you are thinking in terms of Reformed preparationism. So would you show me, from

---

[89] This, of course, does not mean that believers live independently of the word of God. See my *Christ* pp255-256.

[90] Your use of the law is radically different to Paul's occasional use of it (Rom. 13:8-10; 1 Cor. 5:6-8; 9:7-14; Gal. 5:13-15; Eph. 6:1-3).

[91] Murray p166.

Scripture, one pagan who was convicted of his sin, made fit for Christ and led to him by the law of Moses? Will you show me, from Scripture, any preacher who preached the law to pagans?

Again, you have a heading: 'The New Testament and the commandment'.[92] By this, you mean the fourth commandment, of course, and you imply that the New Testament enforces the fourth commandment on believers. Would you give me the reference, please?

Again, take Romans 3:31. Yes, as you say,[93] the gospel really does establish the law, but certainly not in the sense you understand it. The gospel does not impose the law on believers. That wouldn't establish it! Christ by his active obedience under the law (Gal. 4:4-5), by being cursed under the law (Gal. 3:10-14), earned and merited salvation for the elect on the basis of the law; namely, that he who does the law lives (Lev. 18:5; Rom. 10:5). In other words, Christ kept the law, fulfilled the law, and, under the law, merited eternal salvation for his people. It is through the law that the believer has died in Christ to the law (Rom. 7:4; Gal. 2:19). Hence Christ, the gospel, God, has established the law. Let me state that again: Christ kept the law perfectly, bore all its penalty, appeased and satisfied its every demand thereby vindicating his Father's justice and holiness to perfection. This is certainly 'establishing the law'!

There is another point in connection with Romans 3:31. As I said in my letter, you certainly come close to suggesting that those of us who disagree with the Reformed view of the law are verging on antinomianism. The fact is, however, the boot is on the other foot! Reformed covenant-theologians think they establish the law by advocating, with Calvin, the law as a whip to lash believers into sanctification, while, when the going gets tough, using one of the clutch of escape routes they have invented to circumvent the 'awkward' bits of the law. It really won't do! In all this, it is Reformed covenant-theologians who undermine the law. It is they who fail to establish it. They actually *change* it! And even then they are not done: they beaver away finding ways round their new-fangled law, trying to excuse their falling short of it!

---

[92] Murray p152.
[93] Murray p157.

Again, take your reference to Romans 7:22.[94] You take it for granted that this are the words of a spiritual man rejoicing in the ten commandments. Would you prove this, please?[95]

Again, you quote Mathew 5:17.[96] Alas, you miss the point of Christ's reference to 'fulfilment'. Romans 10:4 points to the proper understanding of this important word.[97]

You quote Isaiah 58:13-14,[98] and apply it to the believer, keeping the sabbath literal (though, of course, you change the actual day). Will you be consistent? Do you think 'the temple' and 'the law' of Isaiah 2:1-4 and Micah 4:1-5, the 'clean water' and 'the heart of flesh' of Ezekiel 36:24-27, the 'fountain' of Zechariah 13:1, 'the Feast of Tabernacles', the sacrificial vessels and 'altar' and temple of Zechariah 14:16-21, are literal, too? If not, why not?

Finally, in your setting out of the law written on the heart in the new covenant,[99] you again beg the question by assuming this to be a reference to the ten commandments. Along with this, you assume 'the law of liberty' (Jas. 1:25) is the law of Moses.[100] How that can possibly be true in view of Acts 15:10; 2 Cor. 3:7-11; Gal. 4:21 – 5:1, for instance, defeats me! As for the law written on the believer's heart in the new covenant, it is a very serious question you beg here, one which demands far more care than you give it. In my *Christ is All*,[101] I have set out my reasons for understanding this law as the law of Christ, and not the law of Moses. As I have said, believers are in the realm of the Spirit, not the letter.[102] The law, the letter, which is not of faith (Gal. 3:12), but is the law of sin and death – from which the believer has been set free (Rom. 8:2), which is the killing letter, the ministry of death and

---

[94] Murray p158.

[95] See my *Psalm 119 and the New Covenant*, Brachus, 2014, pp57-61.

[96] Murray 159.

[97] For more. See my *Christ* pp96,170,236-241,498-500.

[98] Murray p149.

[99] Murray pp158-159.

[100] Murray p159.

[101] My *Christ* pp299-321,543-555.

[102] Let me repeat an earlier note: This, of course, does not mean that believers live independently of the word of God. As I say, see my *Christ* pp255-256.

condemnation (2 Cor.3:7-9),[103] this law, this letter, cannot possibly be the law which is written on the believer's heart in the new covenant. I would like to see your scriptural counter-arguments.

National sabbath observance

You argue vehemently for *national* observance of the sabbath,[104] based on the idea that sabbath observance is obligatory and beneficial for all mankind. You want the governments of the UK, America, Australia and all the rest to enforce sabbath observance.

Scripture is explicit that the sabbath was the special distinguishing marker for Israel under the old covenant.[105] You admit it.[106] So would you explain how it is that the special distinguishing old-covenant marker for Israel becomes an essential observance for the believer, a member of the new covenant? How incongruous is the thought! Children of the new covenant having to observe the 'sign' of the old covenant! You might just as well tell them to keep the feasts, new moons, and sacrifices! It is the same as before: believers are in the realm of the Spirit, not the letter.

Would you further explain how the distinguishing sign of the old covenant for Israel comes to be a day of national observance by all the peoples of the world? You have turned the Bible on its head!

By applying the sabbath to non-Jews, Iain, you are driving a coach and horses through these vital biblical principles. Your call for national observance, today, and by all nations, is quite wrong. Having said something on the appalling – mind-boggling –

---

[103] Of which the ten commandment are a part (2 Cor. 3:7).

[104] Murray pp160-169.

[105] As before, this question of the sabbath as the special sign by which God marked Israel in the time of the old covenant is so important because it encapsulates most, if not all, the biblical arguments against universal sabbatarianism. I have devoted Appendix 2 to it. I ask that you read what I have said there.

[106] Murray p147. But, as I have pointed out already, even here you do so in a loaded way: 'The special day became a covenant sign of God's saving work in their midst (Ex. 31:16; Ezek. 20:12)'. Which version of the Bible are you using? I have yet more to say on this extract.

difficulties of enforced national observance of the sabbath, at this point I concentrate on noting the wrongness, the biblical wrongness, of the idea. It is utterly contrary to Scripture, where the sabbath clearly was confined to Israel under the old covenant. It never was intended for universal, national observance in the age of the new covenant.

Let me close, if I may, with a respectful warning. With your talk of 'national observance of the sabbath', Iain, you are in danger of repeating a dreadful mistake that has been made time and again, one which carries dire consequences in its train.[107]

The giving of the manna in Exodus

Iain, you are quite mistaken in your view of this important episode.[108] I simply cannot understand how you can misread the obvious here.

As you say, when God told Moses about the double portion on the sixth day (Ex. 16:4-5), 'the text just quoted gives no explanation why, on the sixth day, twice the amount of manna

---

[107] You get far too close for (my) comfort to regarding (or leading others to regard) 'the nation' (of Scotland, England or whatever) as special – indeed, as Israel – in that you speak as though the nation is under the law of God. Too many believes today are dabbling with this kind of thing. As you know, the damage which such talk has inflicted upon thousands, and the carnage it has unleashed, has been immense. In the 16th and 17th centuries, 'Richard Fitz had thought of England as favoured Israel; while King Edward, more than a decade before Fitz, had regarded the English as the chosen people of God. John Aylmer had taught that "God is English"! Elizabethan Presbyterians like Thomas Cartwright had asserted that... [there] was "a virtual covenant... set up between God and England"... John Field... claimed that God had given himself to the English as a people... John Milton could say God's usual practice was to make his will known "first to his Englishmen". To the Puritans, England was the most favoured nation on earth, the very Israel of God. Many Scots, likewise... As Samuel Rutherford put it: "Now, O Scotland, God be thanked, thy name is in the Bible"; taking the place of Israel, he meant' (I quote from my *Battle for the Church, 1517-1644*, second edition, Brachus, Biggleswade, 2013, pp409-413). I go on to trace the same kind of talk in the 20th century. It is still with us. There is a great deal more that might be said about this, but I leave it there.

[108] Murray pp144-145.

would be given'. As you also say, Moses told the people on the seventh day, with regard to the manna they had kept overnight: 'Eat it today, for today is a sabbath' (Ex. 16:25). And as you further say: 'Some, not believing the word of God, and wanting [expecting, I (DG) would say] manna every day, ignored the command of God, and went out to collect it'. As you say, 'they found none'. And, as you say, God had issued this command to 'test them, whether they will walk in my law or not'. So far, excellent. Then you ask:

How could this be a test unless direction regarding the seventh day had not been already given? Nothing in Exodus 16 suggests that the appointment of a special seventh day of rest was only now being introduced.

I am staggered that you can come to such a manifestly false conclusion.

We can, with precision, date sabbath observance among men – and then only by the Jews; it started at the same time as the giving of the manna in the wilderness soon after the exodus of the Hebrews from Egypt. This is when the sabbath for man began (Ex. 16:22-26). Indeed, not only did this occasion mark the origin among men of the sabbath, the seventh-day rest, but it was the first time the word *sabbath* was ever used.

Let me trace it out. The events surrounding the giving of the manna show that the Hebrews were totally unacquainted with the sabbath before this time. They put it beyond doubt! When the people grumbled about their lack of food and longed for Egypt again, God promised Moses he would provide bread for them. He told Moses what would happen – including the double gathering on the sixth day – and explained his purpose: 'That I may test them, whether they will walk in my law or not' (Ex. 16:1-5). And, as he said, so it happened; the manna fell, and the Israelites gathered it, even though they had never seen it before and did not know what it was. Remarkably, they found the quantity they gathered was just enough for each day's need, but on the sixth day, to their surprise they gathered double the amount. Their amazement drove them back to Moses to tell him what had happened – 'the rulers of the congregation came and reported this to Moses' (Ex. 16:13-22). The Hebrews were utterly flummoxed by the double portion; they didn't have a clue why they had gathered the extra manna, nor what they were supposed to do with it. What was it all about? Why should the Lord give double on the sixth day? Wouldn't it breed maggots like all the other days?

Moses explained: the seventh day, the next day, was to be a ceasing day, 'a sabbath rest', and there would be no manna to collect that day, so that the Hebrews could – and should – rest. The extra collected on the sixth day would not – unlike any kept overnight on other days – breed maggots. Clearly, it was all a novelty to the Hebrews. So much so, at least some of the people didn't grasp the point the first time, or else they were guilty of rank disobedience – and they broke God's law, in that they didn't keep the portion for the seventh day but tried to gather it on the sabbath. Consequently, Moses had to go over it once more from first principles, and tell them that the seventh day was to be a day of rest (Ex 16:23-27).

Now the whole business was so new, the Israelites called the bread 'manna' for that very reason. 'What is it?' they asked. They simply did not know what it was. They had never seen it before. Nobody had. 'And Moses said to them: "This is the bread which the LORD has given you to eat"'. 'And the house of Israel called its name manna' (Ex. 16:15,31); that is, they called it: 'What?' And just as Moses had to explain the ins-and-outs of the manna, so with the sabbath. They had never met it before. Nobody had. The two – the manna and the sabbath – were inextricably linked, and both were equally unknown to the people (Ex. 16:15-31). Years later, Moses twice reminded the Hebrews that God had given them 'manna which you did not know nor did your fathers know' (Deut. 8:3,16). The same might well be said of the sabbath. Thus, they ate bread which they had not known before, and rested on a ceasing day which they had not known before. It constituted one episode.

In fact, when we read that just as 'the children of Israel ate manna forty years, until they came to an inhabited land; they ate manna until they came to the border of the land of Canaan' (Ex. 16:35), I get the impression that unless God had set the sabbath in stone on Sinai, it would have ceased when the manna did. But, of course, at Sinai the sabbath was set in stone. So, while the manna was a temporary expedient to meet Israel's need in the wilderness, the sabbath was not. The sabbath was a permanent part of the old covenant for the Jews, and lasted until Christ. Nevertheless, the two, manna and sabbath, were inextricably linked in Exodus. And not only there. On their return from captivity, the levites took the Israelites over the same ground, making exactly the same point: the sabbath and the manna were given by God at the same time in the desert (Neh. 9:13-15).

It all points one way: in the wilderness, the Hebrews were being *introduced* to the sabbath. God was giving them his law to see if they would keep it or not (Ex. 16:4); *giving* them his law, initiating them into an entirely new commandment and regime, giving them a totally new day and experience, certainly not reminding them of something they knew very well. They had to be told – not reminded! – that the seventh day was the sabbath: 'On the seventh day, the sabbath' (Ex. 16:26). From all this, it is inconceivable that the Hebrews had experienced centuries (millennia) of sabbath keeping. Everything points to the fact that it was an entirely new experience for them. The context gives a invincible proof (sic) that the sabbath was until that time completely unknown to the Israelites.

As for those who try to argue that God was restating the sabbath because the Jews had forgotten it in Egypt, they should note how God, through Ezekiel, complained that Israel desecrated the sabbath in the desert (after Sinai) (Ezek. 20:13-26). If they had forgotten it while in Egypt, why did God not complain about it in Exodus 16?

Note the 'for' in : 'Eat it today, *for* today is a sabbath'. In other words, not only do we now come across the first mention of the sabbath for man – indeed, the first mention of it in all Scripture – but we see Moses giving Israel an explanation of the new day they had just begun. As for the command which they disobeyed, this was not some imaginary command (of which we never read) dating from Genesis 2, but the command just issued, as you yourself quoted. They 'ignored the command of God, and went out to collect it': 'Behold, I will rain bread from heaven for you... on the sixth day... it will be twice as much as they gather daily... [The seventh day] is a sabbath... Today you will not find it in the field.

Six days you shall gather it, but on the seventh day,[109] the sabbath, there will be none'. Here is the command you talk about. And this – not some supposed Genesis-command – the one just given by Moses, is the one the people broke. As I say, I am amazed that you fail to see this.

There are other noteworthy features in this episode: in his explanation of the sabbath, Moses did not refer to creation. He did not refer to God's rest on the seventh day. He did not say: 'As you well know, God commanded Adam to keep this day'. Nor did he refer to that which is supposed to have been ingrained by a weekly practice over centuries. He did not say: 'This is the day men have been keeping since creation'. Nor did he say: 'This is the day which all men should have been keeping since creation'. He did not 'remind' the Hebrews that this was the day their fathers had kept for nearly 2000 years. All this is of the highest significance. To judge by sabbatarians, it was the very thing Moses should have done – the obvious thing. When they asked him what it was all about, he should have dismissed the quibbling Jews, he *would* have dismissed them,[110] retorting that they were wasting his time with such a daft question, pointing out that ever since creation their ancestors – indeed, all men – had been keeping (or failing to keep) the sabbath! Obviously they had not. Everything about the episode cries out that this signalled the introduction of the sabbath among the Jews. Exodus 16, not Genesis 2, marks the origin of sabbath observance among men.

Finally, and by way of introduction to the following section, what do you make of the events of Exodus 15:25-26, just before Elim (Ex. 15:27), whence the Israelites set out for 'the Desert (or Wilderness) of Sin, which is between Elim and Sinai' (Ex. 16:1)? Let me quote the passage:

There [at Marah] the LORD made a decree and a law for them, and there he tested them. He said: 'If you listen carefully to the voice of the LORD your God and do what is right in his eyes, if you pay attention to his commands and keep all his decrees, I will not bring on

---

[109] Do not miss the repeated explanation – it was all so new to them.

[110] Moses was not averse to rebuking the Israelites for their stupidity (and worse), telling them home truths. See Ex. 17:2; 32:21,30; Num. 14:41, for instance.

you any of the diseases I brought on the Egyptians, for I am the LORD, who heals you' (Ex. 15:25-26).

As I say, what do you make of it? To me it has all the appearance of a kind of preface to what was going to happen in the Wilderness of Sin and, supremely, at Sinai; namely, the giving of the law – in particular, the sabbath. This is strengthened by what we read of events the closer Israel got to Sinai: 'They entered the Desert of Sinai, and Israel camped there in the desert in front of the mountain. Then Moses went up to God, and the LORD called to him from the mountain and said':

This is what you are to say to the house of Jacob and what you are to tell the people of Israel: 'You yourselves have seen what I did to Egypt, and how I carried you on eagles' wings and brought you to myself. Now if you obey me fully and keep my covenant, then out of all nations you will be my treasured possession. Although the whole earth is mine, you will be for me a kingdom of priests and a holy nation'. These are the words you are to speak to the Israelites (Ex. 19:2-6).

The rest of that chapter is taken up with this very emphasis: God is going to give his law, his covenant, to Israel; Israel must obey; and the people respond to God by promising obedience.

All this serves to confirm the fact that the Wilderness of Sin leading to Sinai really does mark both the time and the place of the giving of the law (including, of course, the sabbath) to Israel. Nothing could be clearer: God did not give the sabbath to Adam!

The giving of the law at Sinai

You refer to the word 'remember' in the fourth commandment, and go on to deduce that this 'confirms that the sabbath was not new but already existing. The commandment does not begin: "Know there is a sabbath day", but: "*Remember...*"' and this 'is specifically identified with Genesis 2:3'.[111] You claim this is a call to the Jews to remember the sabbath because they knew the Lord had blessed the sabbath day at creation, instituting it as a weekly rest day for men.

---

[111] Murray p145, emphasis yours.

But this is not necessarily so. In fact, it is not so. As I have pointed out, the sabbath is not mentioned in Genesis, and the blessing of Genesis 2 refers to the ultimate rest for the people of God, not the weekly seventh-day observance among the Jews which would begin, centuries later, in the wilderness before Sinai. What is more, the command to 'remember', if it is a backward look, does not refer to creation, but to the establishment of the day for the Jews at the giving of the manna in Exodus 16, a few weeks earlier. In fact, the word 'remember' may not be referring back at all. I will deal with this a little later.

In Exodus 20, God was making an analogy with *his* rest after creation. After all, in Deuteronomy 5:15, the supporting argument was Israel's deliverance from Egypt. Both references were analogies: 'Just as God rested after his work of creation, so you must rest after your work; God rescued you from the enslaving toils of Egypt, therefore you must rest'. See also Exodus 31:12-18; 35:1-3; Deuteronomy 5:12-15. In this latter passage, the giving again of the law, where the reference was not to creation but to the release of the Jews from Egypt, note the 'therefore' in verse 15. In other words: 'This is why the Lord commanded you to keep the sabbath': you must keep the sabbath *because* he released you from Egypt.

This is important. Should Gentile sabbatarians today keep the sabbath in memory of, and because of, their release from Egypt? Or the release of the Jews from Egypt? What redemption or salvation are pagans commemorating when they keep the sabbath? Do they know it? Should they know it?

Further, it has been suggested that the 'therefore' in Exodus 20:11 is best understood as 'after this', 'consequently now', not as a command to remember a creation ordinance: 'In six days the LORD made the heavens and the earth, the sea, and all that is in them, but he rested on the seventh day. Therefore [after this, consequently now] the LORD blessed the sabbath day and made it holy'.

Above all, Iain, although you claim that the word 'remember' points back to a previously known truth, this is not necessarily so. As a matter of fact, it is highly unlikely. Take, for instance, an anxious mother's injunction to her departing child, leaving home for the first time: 'Remember to wrap up warm in the cold weather!' Or to that child off to a party: 'Remember to say thank you'. The command to 'remember the sabbath' was God's call to the Jews not to forget it in the future, but to keep it. Take Christ's injunction to his disciples: 'Remember the word that I said to you...' (John 15:20). In other words: 'Do it!' And this: 'Remember Lot's wife!' (Luke 17:32); that is: 'Learn from her disobedience, never forget it, and never repeat it'.

Scripture often uses the word in this way. As we do. The word 'remember' at its root has the idea of 'marking'; it means 'call to mind, keep in mind'.[112] When Elihu told Job to 'remember to magnify [God's] work' (Job 36:24), he was telling him not to forget this duty *in the future*, not to let it lapse. When the psalmist appealed to God: 'Remember how short my time is' (Ps. 89:47), he was asking God to keep it in mind in his dealings with him *in the days to come*. The same goes for Psalm 106:4: 'Remember me, O LORD, with the favour you have toward your people'. God remembered both Noah and Hannah (Gen. 8:1; 1 Sam. 1:19); that is, he thought on them for good, he kept them in mind. What did the malefactor want when he begged Christ: 'Jesus, remember me when you come into your kingdom' (Luke 23:42)? Was he asking the Lord to remember the agony of the cross, or what? When Paul asked the Colossians to 'remember [his] chains' (Col. 4:18), he wanted them to keep his sufferings in mind and him in their prayers. He was afraid they would forget him as time passed; a case of 'out of sight, out of mind'. He was not making a historical point. It was the present and the future he was thinking of. The same goes for: 'Remember the prisoners as if chained with them' (Heb. 13:3). In short, the word 'remember' has a *future* emphasis. Indeed, it is its *main* emphasis.

We may go further. The command to 'remember' means more than 'do not forget'. It has the sense of 'observe and celebrate'. I draw your attention to the parallel passage to Exodus 20:8 – Deuteronomy 5:12 – which actually does use 'observe'. When Christ instituted the Lord's supper, he told his disciples to 'do this

---

[112] In Yorkshire (in the UK), if a mother tells her child: 'Think on!' she is really saying: 'Remember what I told you. *And do it!*' Compare: 'Mind your P's and Q's!'

in remembrance of me' (Luke 22:19). This presents us with a very powerful parallel with the 'remember' in the fourth commandment. Just as Christ was instituting his supper when he said it, so God was *instituting* the sabbath. Christ was *instituting* the supper; it did not exist before.

Sabbath observance had not existed for centuries (and more) when God *instituted* the sabbath at Sinai (confirming what he had introduced in the Wilderness of Sin). It was through Moses that God established the sabbath for Israel (in Exodus 16), and set it in stone (in Exodus 20). And it was based on Israel's deliverance from Egypt, their rest in Canaan, and had a powerful resonance with God's own rest after creation.

The parallel between the supper and the sabbath merits a further look. In both cases, there was (for the sabbath) and is (for the supper) an in-built endpoint. From the time of Christ's institution of the supper, believers have had to observe it, and will do so as long as its remit runs – until Christ's second coming. Likewise, the Jews had to observe the sabbath as long as its remit ran – until Christ had come, fulfilled the law, rendered it obsolete, and thus established the new covenant: 'The law... was added... *until* the Seed [Christ] to whom the promise referred had come' (Gal. 3:19). The Lord Jesus has come and done it all (John 19:30); the law is fulfilled (Rom. 6:14-15; 7:1-6; 8:1-4; 10:4; Heb. 7:18; 8:13). As the sabbath was in force under the law *until* its fulfilment and abrogation by Christ, so the supper has to be observed by believers *until* his return. In both cases, this is what 'remember' means. Just as the supper will not be observed once Christ has returned, so the sabbath has had no purpose since Christ established the new covenant.[113]

---

[113] Old-covenant observance did not cease at a stroke. There is clear New Testament evidence that grey areas existed for a time. See for example Acts 21:17-26. Nevertheless, just as the temple veil was torn down (Matt. 27:51), so, in reality, the temple, the sacrifices, the altar, the temple, the priesthood all came to an end, all having been fulfilled and abolished by Christ. The sabbath is not the sole exception to this principle. The fact that the apostles used the sabbath to evangelise the Jews, does not mean they were sabbatarians. Just as Jesus, eating with prostitutes and profligates, did not become one, neither did Paul become a sabbatarian by attending

Finally, let me take you back to the Passover. I refer to Exodus 13:3-10. God commanded the people to celebrate, to keep, to observe, the Passover every year. As the NIV puts it: 'Commemorate this day, the day you came out of Egypt, out of the land of slavery, because the LORD brought you out of it with a mighty hand... You must keep this ordinance at the appointed time year after year' (Ex. 13:3,10). 'Commemorate', please note, and 'you must keep...'. It is interesting to see how other versions translate this:

Remember this day in which you came out from Egypt, out of the house of slavery, for by a strong hand the LORD brought you out from this place... You shall therefore keep this statute at its appointed time from year to year (ESV).
Remember this day in which you went out from Egypt, from the house of slavery; for by a powerful hand the LORD brought you out from this place... Therefore, you shall keep this ordinance at its appointed time from year to year (NASB).
Remember this day, in which [you] came out from Egypt, out of the house of bondage; for by strength of hand the LORD brought you out from this place... [You shall] therefore keep this ordinance in his season from year to year (AV).

In fact, this translation ('remember') is almost universal. Putting it all together, the NIV has done us a good service in this text. Clearly, the main point is one of Israel's remembrance of their deliverance from Egypt by way of commemoration, by their continual observance of the feast.[114] And the same was true of the sabbath. The Jews, keeping the day, should have used it as a weekly reminder of their deliverance from Egypt (parallel to their annual remembrance at the Passover). Above all, if only they had had eyes and hearts to see it, every sabbath they were being pointed to the rest to be introduced by the coming Messiah in the salvation he would accomplish.

---

the synagogue or going to a meeting by the river (Acts 13:5,14; 14:1; 16:13, and so on). He went to preach the gospel!
[114] See also Deut. 16:1-8.

The testimony of the Fathers

You are pleased to be able to cite the Fathers in defence of the so-called Christian sabbath (so-called by men, but never in Scripture).[115] You give the impression that the Fathers' contribution is clear cut. But it is not. Far from it! Not everybody is agreed about exactly what some of the early Fathers meant, are they? Some contest – and contest strongly – that the Fathers were sabbatarians, and they have evidence for it, certainly among the very early Fathers.[116] Again, many talk as though the Fathers spoke with one voice. But this they certainly did not do! Not only were they ambiguous at times, and self-contradictory, but they quarrelled among themselves; there were battles royal among the various factions at the time. And, as always, history is written by the winners. Nor is it always remembered that the Fathers spanned at least four centuries. Then again, we have the eastern and the western Fathers, not forgetting the incredible array of 'heretics' of all shades of opinion. In short, it is probably safe to say that he who takes the sword of the Fathers to make a theological point will nearly always end up cutting himself in the process.

Nevertheless, let it stand: the Fathers were sabbatarians. But then we expected that. After all, they went to the old covenant (sometimes even to the pagans), without biblical warrant, to devise many of the corruptions which plague the Church to this day: buildings, priestcraft, pastorcraft, clergy, sacerdotalism, sacramentalism, vestments, ordination, apostolic succession, *etc.*

---

[115] Who was the first to call Sunday 'the Christian sabbath'? If it is true that the first mention of Sunday as a day of rest can be found in Origen in AD220, does that mark the origin of 'the Christian sabbath'? Or do we have to look to the English Puritans for it?

[116] Ignatius, for instance: 'Do not be deceived by strange doctrines or antiquated myths, since they are worthless. For if we continue to live in accordance with Judaism, we admit that we have not received grace... If, then, those who had lived in antiquated practices came to newness of hope, no longer keeping the sabbath but living in accordance with the Lord's day, on which our life also arose through him and his death...' (*To the Magnesians*). Eusebius: 'They did not, therefore, regard circumcision, nor observe the sabbath, neither do we... because such things as these do not belong to Christians' (*Ecclesiastical History*).

Do you advocate any or all of these things? And do you like this from Eusebius, whom you quoted: 'All things that it was the duty to do on the sabbath, these have we transferred to the Lord's day...'?[117] *We* have transferred...? *All* things... transferred?

Taking up the point about 'we [the Fathers] have transferred': at least, Eusebius was honest. As you know, you cannot quote Christ or the apostles for changing the sabbath from the seventh to the first day. No! So who was responsible? This of course involves a change in the law of God. What, therefore, I wonder, do you think of these words:

Do not add to what I command you and do not subtract from it, but keep the commands of the LORD your God that I give you (Deut. 4:2).
See that you do all I command you; do not add to it or take away from it (Deut. 12:32).
Be careful to obey all the law my servant Moses gave you; do not turn from it to the right or to the left... Meditate on it day and night, so that you may be careful to do everything written in it (Josh. 1:7-8).

In light of such clear warnings, do you have any apprehension about observing the sabbath under a change in the unchangeable law of God, a change produced by nobody knows who?

And, speaking of 'all things' being 'transferred' (including the prohibition of any work), may I ask if you do any work at all, on what you call the sabbath? Especially, I ask, do you light a fire (or the equivalent)? I raise this, of course, because, as you yourself (in part) quote,[118] Moses was explicit:

Observe the sabbath, because it is holy to you. Anyone who desecrates it must be put to death; whoever does any work on that day must be cut off from his people. For six days, work is to be done, but the seventh day is a sabbath of rest, holy to the LORD. Whoever does any work on the sabbath day must be put to death (Ex.31:14-15; see also Ex. 20:10; 35:1-3; Lev. 23:3; Deut. 5:14; and so on).
These are the things the LORD has commanded you to do: For six days, work is to be done, but the seventh day shall be your holy day, a sabbath of rest to the LORD. Whoever does any work on it must be

---

[117] Murray p155.
[118] Murray p147.

62

put to death. Do not light a fire in any of your dwellings on the sabbath day (Ex. 35:1-3).

And however you interpret 'a sabbath day's walk' (Acts 1:12), which the NIV footnote defines as 1100 metres, bearing in mind Exodus 16:29-30, may I ask if you keep to the rule?

May I also ask how it is that, on what you and the Banner call the sabbath, people can purchase a copy of your *Evangelical Holiness* (in which they are able to read your strictures on breaking the sabbath) through the Banner of Truth website? If it is not possible to take the site down for the sacred 24 hours, why don't you, at the very least, set up a dialogue box warning prospective purchasers that they are endangering their immortal souls by proceeding with the purchase before midnight on Sunday, and asking if they really wish to proceed?[119]

While speaking of the Fathers, may I ask you to tell me the first man in Scripture who kept the Lord's day as a day of rest? As you know you have to go to the Fathers for that. You cannot tell me of any such talk in the New Testament. What is the earliest date for fixing the Lord's day as a day of rest among the Fathers? As far as I understand it, it came into law with the edict of Constantine in AD321, although, as I have noted, I have read that it first appears in the works of Origen in AD220. I ask all this, of course, because of its importance, since 'sabbath' and 'rest' are synonymous.[120] You have no *biblical* warrant for calling the Lord's day the sabbath. And as for the early Fathers, it would appear that they

---

[119] Pleading Westminster's phrase, 'works of necessity and mercy' won't do, even though it must be a prime candidate to win the competition to discover the most elastic phrase in the English language. While there was such an old-covenant provision when the sabbath was in force among the Jews (Luke 13:15; 14:5), the way the Reformed use it, as a contrivance to get round proper sabbath observance, would be highly amusing – *if the matter were not so serious*.

[120] You, yourself, speak freely of 'the day of rest' (Murray pp144-152, for instance), and you use 'sabbath' and 'Lord's day' as interchangeable throughout your work. Indeed in your quote from Abraham Kuyper you state: 'On the Lord's day... on that day of rest...' (Murray p143). And the title of your work says it all: 'Rest in God: The Fourth Commandment *is* for Today'. So as to leave no misunderstanding, all I am asking is that you give me the *scripture* to establish this link.

knew nothing of it. So who did start it? Of course, once the corruption had been introduced, as with so much else, the later Fathers, leading to the Medieval Church, and so to the Reformers, developed it with vigour.

Widening your sources still further, your section: 'The witness of history', and on to the end of your work,[121] proves nothing other than that Reformed men down the centuries have held your view. I think we knew that. This section of your work offers no proof, however, that Christian sabbatarianism is biblical.

Indeed, I think these sane words, written by Kenneth L.Parker, should be weighed by all sabbatarians:

In the first three centuries of Christianity, theologians like Irenaeus, Justin, and Tertullian... [interpreted] the sabbath precept as a spiritual rest from sin. But during the fourth century, this allegorical interpretation gave way to an analogical explanation, with theologians applying the sabbath laws... to the Christian Sunday... The application of Jewish sabbath laws remained an important part of medieval justifications for strict Sunday observance... However... 13th century scholastic theologians introduced a new explanation... The scholastics discarded the allegorical and analogical interpretations... defining instead the moral and ceremonial parts of this law. Thomas Aquinas... explained that... by [the sabbath] men were firmly established in genuine religion... Aquinas' position was to be crucial for all subsequent development of sabbatarianism... He... explained that the day had been shifted from the Jewish sabbath to the Christian Sunday... This Thomistic distinction between the moral and ceremonial parts of the sabbath precept was accepted by nearly all subsequent sabbatarian writers.[122]

As you yourself demonstrate, Iain.

---

[121] Murray pp160-169.

[122] Kenneth L.Parker: *The English Sabbath...*, Cambridge University Press, Cambridge, 1988, pp17-20. For finer tuning, consider P.Gerard Damsteegt's review of John H.Primus: *Holy Time: Moderate Puritanism and the Sabbath*, Mercer University Press, Macon, 1989. Damsteegt: Primus 'highlights certain emphases which Parker tends to overlook... By the end of the sixteenth century "sabbatarianism had become the linchpin in the Puritan programme for more complete reform in England", with one of its distinguishing characteristics being "the divine appointment of Sunday as the new day of rest"' (andrews.edu).

Parker puts all this sabbatarianism into its proper context. Sabbatarians should recognise that they are the children of the Fathers and the scholastics, Thomas Aquinas in particular, and not, in this regard, children of the new covenant. They should be honest with themselves and admit that Scripture says nothing about their sabbatarianism – except to condemn both it (Gal. 4:10; Col. 2:16-17) and their insistence on the observance of the (invented) sabbath by other believers (Rom. 14:5-12). Furthermore, they should recognise that men, starting with the Fathers, through the scholastics, and then the Reformers, have been forever tinkering with their sabbatarian system. They are still at it. If not a 'moveable feast', at the very least 'the Christian sabbath' seems to be of the 'slippery' or 'pliable' variety.

Calvin's testimony

You call upon John Calvin, and try to get him to speak in your support. OK. Let's take a look at Calvin.

First of all, it is necessary to remember that he, like all the magisterial Reformers, was a Medieval man, and, as such, had very heavily imbibed the teaching of the Fathers. Furthermore, it is his view of the law which has dominated the Reformed faith these past 450 years. So it would be hardly surprising to find him to have been a firm sabbatarian. One would have expected it. But, of course, that is precisely what he was not! As you know, this stubborn fact has been an acute embarrassment for all Reformed writers since the time of the Puritans, when Reformed sabbatarianism first reared its head in England.

The fact is, clearly you yourself don't like it.[123] So I can well understand why you are eager to try (but in vain) to clear Calvin's statements in his *Institutes*.[124] Nevertheless, I fully accept your point about Calvin's later *Sermons* and *Commentaries*. So let us agree that Calvin, like us all, was guilty of inconsistency and self-contradiction. Sadly, however, you seem to be tarred with the same

---

[123] By the way, do you have any tinge of embarrassment at Calvin's picture of believers, like lazy asses, having to be whipped by the law in order to be sanctified?

[124] Murray pp150-152.

brush as a good many other Reformed men in that you cannot actually bring yourself to admit Calvin's inconsistencies. Instead, you talk in terms of the 'variations of emphasis in Calvin's thought'.[125] Why not say it straight out? Calvin, as all of us, was guilty of a measure of inconsistency and self-contradiction. After all, since he wrote, preached and published a huge amount, spread over many years, it would be staggering if he had not made any progress during that time, and changed his mind. And, as I say, and like us all, he was not always consistent.

More seriously over this issue of inconsistency on the sabbath between the *Institutes* and his other works, there are three points I would like you to address:

1. As you yourself admit,[126] Calvin was prepared to revise his *Institutes*, and more than once; witness his change on baptism because of his hostility to the Anabaptists. So, if he really had changed his mind on the sabbath, why did he not revise the *Institutes* yet again? If he had become a full-blown sabbatarian, knowing, as he did, the severity of the law against sabbath breaking, whyever did he not make sure that his *Institutes*, which he regarded as definitive (and which he must have known were having a wide influence), reflected his mature and settled view?

2. Calvin *was* explicit that the *Institutes* constituted his final word on all matters – not his *Commentaries*:

I have endeavoured [here in the *Institutes*] to give such a summary of religion in all its parts... Having thus... paved the way, I shall not feel it necessary, in any *Commentaries* on Scripture which I may afterwards publish, to enter into long discussions of doctrine... In this way, the pious reader will be saved much trouble and weariness, provided he comes furnished with a knowledge of the [*Institutes*] as an essential prerequisite... seeing that I have in a manner deduced at length all the articles which pertain to Christianity.[127]

---

[125] Murray p152.
[126] Murray p150.
[127] Calvin: *Institutes* in his prefixed explanations for the work dated 1539 and 1545.

You think very highly of Calvin. As I do. Why, therefore, don't you take him at his word?

3. Would you not agree that Calvin is signally weak at a key point in this debate? I refer to his argument for the biblical change of the sabbath to the first day of the week. As far as I know, Calvin never argued for the change of the sabbath to the first day of the week; no, not in his *Institutes*, *Sermons* or *Commentaries*. But I stand to be corrected on this. Perhaps you would give Calvin's biblical justification for that important change (if indeed he did offer one)? Important? It is vital! Can you give us references to show that Calvin asserted that the Lord's day is the sabbath? So as to leave no misunderstanding, I am not asking about Calvin's argument that the early churches met on the first day of the week – I have no doubt about that – but I am concerned to know Calvin's view on the change of the sabbath into the Lord's day, especially whether or not he offers any biblical warrant for it.[128] After all, it constitutes a major change in God's law – which law, he himself called 'one perpetual and inflexible rule'; in other words, unchangeable.[129]

Colossians 2:16-17

Iain, I must say that I find your remarks on Colossians 2:16-17 baffling: 'There is no certainty at all that [these verses] have to do with the keeping of the seventh day'.[130] Whatever else they refer to, these verses undoubtedly do refer to believers and sabbath observance:

---

[128] I cannot see how he can, in light of his comments on Mark 2:27: 'They are mistaken... who suppose that in this passage the sabbath is [was] entirely abolished [at that time]; for Christ simply informs us what is the proper use of it. Though he asserted, a little before, that he is Lord of the sabbath, yet the full time for its abolition [the true season and appropriate time for the abolition of it] was not yet come, because the veil of the temple was not yet rent'. In other words, in establishing the new covenant – 'the true season and appropriate time for the abolition of it' – Christ abolished the sabbath. He could hardly, therefore, argue that the Lord's day is the sabbath.

[129] Calvin: *Institutes* 2.7.13.

[130] Murray pp152-153.

Let no one judge you in food or in drink, or regarding a festival or a new moon or sabbaths, which are a shadow of things to come, but the substance is of Christ.

You go on to say: 'In the ceremonial law there were other "sabbath days"' and so on. 'In the ceremonial law...'!

Here we go again! As I have explained, your threefold division of the law is unwarranted, lacking any scriptural proof, simply assumed and imposed upon Scripture. As you know, the notion came from Thomas Aquinas.[131] In Scripture, the law is the law. That's a general point, though one which is relevant and highly significant. It means that this 'ceremonial law' escape route is not open to you.[132]

Coming to the particular, Paul exhorts the Colossian believers not to let anyone impose any shadow of the old covenant upon them. Believers are not obliged to keep any old-covenant rules and laws concerning diet, feasts or days, including sabbath observance. This is his point. This is what he says.

Let me develop this a little. The 'judging' is almost certainly an act of condemnation, of disapproval, not approval. Paul told the Colossians not to let themselves feel threatened by those who disapproved of their attitude to food, drink, and Jewish days,

---

[131] This is generally assumed. Aquinas certainly systematised it. But whoever was responsible, it wasn't the Holy Spirit in Scripture. See my *Christ* pp100-104,392-400.

[132] Do you think that the fourth commandment is partly moral and partly ceremonial, and so shuffle 'the seventh day' aspect off into the ceremonial, and thus feel free to dispense with it? Parker lists a number of Reformers and Puritans who took that line (Parker pp97-98). If so, as Parker went on, quoting John Sprint's work of 1607: 'However... there were three "points of difference [about this] among the godly learned". These concerned whether keeping the seventh day or any other was part of the moral law, whether the first day of the week was established by divine truth and tied to the conscience, and whether the Lord's day might be changed again to another day'. Which of the three do you prefer? And what are your scriptural grounds for your choice? Don't you think your followers have a right to have this set out fully and clearly? I say this, as always, because the consequences of getting it wrong are severe in the extreme.

including sabbaths, and to let themselves be pressurised into keeping such.

In light of this, to think that Paul would happily countenance, let alone advocate, sabbath keeping, is hard to swallow – especially when he immediately dismisses the practice, calling it by its proper name: a shadow. This is a point of the utmost importance. It is the crux here. What, in this context, is a shadow? The word 'shadow' is used by artists to denote either a rough outline of an object which they mean to draw or paint, or its silhouette. The sabbath was one of several old-covenant shadows of Christ, all of which were fulfilled in him.

And the New Testament is explicit, unequivocal: how wrong it is to give up the substance and go back to the shadow (Col. 2:17). How strongly Scripture speaks against it (Heb. 8:1 – 10:18). It would be akin to offering sacrifices. Consequently, it is unthinkable that Paul should countenance sabbath observance for believers. Believers have Christ, they are in Christ, and Christ is in them – they must not cling to the shadow. This of course is because salvation in Christ is the true and only rest; the sabbath was merely a shadow of it. Who would want the shadow when he has the real thing? To go to the shadow when the reality is here is an insult to God!

Calvin on Exodus 31:17:

The sabbath, although its external observation is not now in use, still remains eternal in its reality, like circumcision. Thus the stability of both was best confirmed by their abrogation; since, if God now required the same of Christians, it would be putting a veil over the death and resurrection of his Son; and hence the more carefully the Jews[133] persevere in the keeping the festival, the more do they derogate from its sanctity. But they calumniate us falsely, as if we disregarded the sabbath; because there is nothing which more completely confirms its reality and substance than the abolition of its external use.[134]

Powerful words! They express my feelings about this question. Iain, what do you say?

---

[133] What Calvin says fits present-day sabbatarians like a glove.

[134] See later extract from Calvin on Heb. 4.

Calvin referred to his *Commentary* on Genesis 17. Commenting on Genesis 17:13, he talked of two shadows: the sabbath and circumcision. He argued that, in each case, Christ brought the external to an end by establishing the spiritual reality. Consequently, Calvin said, 'it would be absurd' to have the reality and, at the same time, keep the shadow: 'The one should testify and affirm that Christ was come, and the other should shadow him forth as absent'. While Calvin was arguing this in terms of circumcision (but clearly including the sabbath),[135] and I disagree with his view of the 'reality' of the rite of circumcision, nevertheless, the point about the sabbath is well made. It *is* 'absurd' to have sabbath rest in Christ, and yet keep the shadow of sabbath observance. Which is precisely what you do. How do you feel when you read Calvin dismissing your position as 'absurd'?

As for the apostle's use of 'sabbaths' in Colossians 2, the plural does not in any way negate the concept of the weekly sabbath; see for instance Exodus 31:13-14. This is borne out by the way in which the various versions translate the plural of Colossians 2:16:

Therefore do not let anyone judge you by what you eat or drink, or with regard to a religious festival, a new moon celebration or **a sabbath day** (NIV).
Therefore let no one pass judgment on you in questions of food and drink, or with regard to a festival or a new moon or **a sabbath** (ESV).
Therefore no one is to act as your judge in regard to food or drink or in respect to a festival or a new moon or **a sabbath day** (NASB).
Let no man therefore judge you in meat, or in drink, or in respect of an holyday, or of the new moon, or of **the sabbath** *days* (AV).[136]

Those versions are right. The Greek lexicons speak of the plural standing for the singular.[137] In other words, when you try to shunt the apostle's words into 'festivals, in addition to the weekly sabbath', you are clinging to a non-existent straw. In any case, even though there were other sabbath festivals, Paul was talking

---

[135] As he did the other way round in Exodus.
[136] The italics means it was added by the translators. Literally the AV reads 'the sabbath'. This is why I have had to highlight in bold.
[137] Compare the strengthening of the concept of 'the law' by the omission of the definite article.

about the whole lot – including the weekly sabbath. All are gone. None should be kept by believers.

Notice further that these verses (Col. 2:16-17) also refer to food and drink, which have nothing whatsoever to do with Christ, 'for the kingdom of God is not food and drink' (Rom. 14:17; 1 Cor. 8:8). In all this, the verses refer to the old covenant – to Jewish festivals, ceremonies, diet and, especially, days – 'a new moon' and 'sabbaths' (2 Kings 4:23; 1 Chron. 23:31; 2 Chron. 2:4; 31:3; Ezra 3:4-5; Neh. 10:32-33; Isa. 1:13-14; Ezek. 45:17; 46:1-6; Hos. 2:11) – things which were 'a shadow' of Christ. They were a part of 'the handwriting of requirements that was against us, which was contrary to us' which has been fulfilled, removed and abolished in Christ (Col. 2:14; see also Eph. 2:15). The only time the new moon is mentioned in the New Testament is here in Colossians 2:16, where we are told it has nothing to do with believers. Believers should keep none of these days, not feast day, new moon or sabbath. This is what Paul was saying. The sabbath (as a day) has been fulfilled and abolished, since it was a shadow representing and pointing forward to Christ, the true sabbath (Heb. 3:7-19; 4:1-11). Believers should not keep the sabbath. Christ is our sabbath. We should not cling to shadows. Nor should we allow anybody to impose them on us. The is the plain teaching of Colossians 2:16-17.

Hebrews 4:9-11

You agree that the law was a shadow, prefiguring Christ – the sabbath prefiguring the believer's rest in Christ. Sadly, however, you can bring yourself to speak only rather grudgingly about it: 'There is an important element of truth here'.[138] Iain, there is rather more than that! In fact, there is a great deal more than that.

I have already commented on your loaded way of talking about the sabbath as God's appointed sign distinguishing Israel under the old covenant:

The sabbath was also at this time related to God's redemptive purposes. It was now a memorial not only of creation but of the nation's deliverance from Egypt (Deut. 5:15). The special day became

---

[138] Murray pp156-157.

a covenant sign of God's saving work in their midst (Ex. 31:16; Ezek. 20:12).[139]

What do I mean by 'loaded'? There are several points. I have already noted that the sabbath did not 'become' a sign; God *instituted* it. Nor was it 'a' sign; it was 'the' sign of the covenant. Furthermore, the sabbath did not change it's hat at Sinai; right from its institution, God established it as the special marker for Israel in the old covenant. Again, the 'redemption' or 'salvation' of Israel was only a shadow of the real salvation in Christ in the new covenant. Deliverance from Egypt was not 'salvation' in the full sense; it was only a shadow of the believer's redemption in Christ, his deliverance from sin, law and death. Everything about Israel's deliverance from Egypt firmly pointed to the reality; namely, Christ.[140]

In God's providence, it fell to the writer to the Hebrews to deal with the sabbath (along with all the other old-covenant shadows), and tell us plainly what it is today. From his letter, we are left in no doubt as to the sabbath's place in the new covenant: it is fulfilled in Christ. The true sabbath is found in him, it is experienced in him, and only in him. Indeed, in the new covenant, the sabbath *is* Christ. Just as Christ is his law,[141] so Christ is the sabbath. Far from being a day of the week to be observed by all mankind, therefore, the sabbath is a spiritual experience which is enjoyed by believers, and my believers only, and enjoyed permanently by them from the moment they trust Christ. Christ is their sabbath; more, he is their all (Col. 3:11). This is the point of Hebrews 3:7 – 4:11. This vital passage in connection with the sabbath in the new covenant, especially Hebrews 4:9-11, demands careful attention. It reads:

---

[139] Murray p147.

[140] I am not not-picking. Such glosses do untold damage because they are so subtle. As a consequence, those who fail to spot them can be steered away from the biblical position. And more so in this way, perhaps, than by a direct assault on the text.

[141] See my *Christ* pp258-261,509-510.

There remains therefore a rest for the people of God. For he who has entered his rest has himself also ceased from his works, as God did from his. Let us therefore be diligent to enter that rest.

There *is* a sabbath – a ceasing, a rest – for saints in the new covenant.

Indeed, Iain, I am unspeakably relieved it is so. If there were no sabbath, no rest for the saints today, believers would be of all men the most miserable. I would. You would. We would still be bound in our sins, engaged in a futile working of an endless treadmill to get ourselves out of bondage into freedom – and always failing. I would. You would. But, praise be to God, the believer *is* at rest, having learned, having been 'taught by God' (Isa. 54:13; Jer. 31:33-34; John 6:45; Heb. 8:8-13; 10:15-18) to cease from his works.

And this is true not only for justification. Sadly, the Reformed try to limit the rest to that. But Scripture shows us plainly that the rest includes assurance which leads to sanctification (and in that order). Both assurance and sanctification are by Christ, through his Spirit, in the gospel – and not by the law. I will not confirm these points here, having done so at length elsewhere.[142]

This rest for believers, therefore, most definitely is *not* a day of the week. It is Christ. The believer must keep his eye on Christ, looking to Christ, listening to the witness of the Spirit taking him to Christ. This is the teaching of Hebrews 4:9-11. This is the real, true sabbath, the only sabbath; namely, the present spiritual rest which is a foretaste of God's purpose culminating in that eternal rest which all the elect will enjoy in and through Christ. As I keeping saying, the sabbath is Christ. The sabbath is the salvation he wrought for his people, the salvation they enjoy at this moment, and above all the eternal rest he is preparing for them. *This* is the true sabbath. *This* is what Hebrews 4:9-11 speaks of. Trying to use the passage to talk about a weekly sabbath under the gospel is tragic. Tragic, I say. Throughout Hebrews, priest, sacrifice and altar are all nuanced into Christ. So why do you persist in making

---

[142] In my *Christ* and in my *Assurance in the New Covenant*, Brachus, 2014.

an exception of the sabbath? On what biblical grounds do you do it?

You raise the question of the person spoken of in Hebrews 4:10. To whom was the sacred writer referring when he said: 'He who has entered his rest has himself also ceased from his works, as God did from his'? Who is the person 'who has entered his rest'? Who is it that has 'ceased from his works'? Amazingly, along with John Owen, you claim Hebrews 4:10 describes *Christ* resting after *his* work of redemption. You do not think the verse is speaking of the unbeliever coming to trust in Christ.[143] You, along with Owen, dismiss this because of the parallel with God ceasing from his *creating* works: the sinner ceases his *sinful* works.[144] Consequently, you say, the writer must be speaking of Christ.

I think not! Taking up your argument, God ceased from his work of *creation*. The works Christ ceased from, the works he finished (John 19:30), were his suffering, sacrificial, atoning, saving works.[145] The parallel breaks down, even on your scheme.

In any case, all this misses the point. It's wide of the mark. You are missing the wood for the trees. The writer is not concerned with the nature of the works, but with the *ceasing*. It is the ceasing which counts – whether God from creation, Christ from saving, or the sinner from trying to be right with God. Rest is the issue! And there is rest 'for *anyone* who enters God's rest, since he 'also rests from his own work' (Heb. 4:10). That is, when we believe in Christ, at that moment *we* enter into rest – *we* are freed from the burden and toil of our sin, *we* are freed from trying to justify ourselves before God, *we* are freed from sin, law, fear and death. And *we* enter into rest. Hebrews 4:3 says so: 'For we who have believed do enter that rest'. This surely speaks of the sinner who believes – not Christ! We enter God's rest by faith (Heb. 3:18-19), by believing (Heb. 4:2-3); to enter this rest is to become one of the

---

[143] Murray p157.

[144] Yes, but, strictly speaking, the sinner ceases from struggling in vain to be right with God.

[145] Continuing in your vein, strictly speaking Paul refers to Christ's '*one* act of righteousness' (Rom. 5:18 – see the NIV, ESV, NASB, rightly reflecting the Greek). The NKJV does not quite catch it; nearly, but not quite. The AV misses it altogether.

'partakers of Christ' (Heb. 3:14). This must be speaking of the sinner who believes, not Christ. Furthermore, it is the disobedience of unbelief which keeps the sinner out of rest (Heb. 3:12-19; 4:1-6), and condemns him (Mark 16:16; John 3:18,36).

Could anything be more clear? Believers can look back and see that as sinners they used to toil in bondage. Whether it was the law, which held them in prison, 'kept under guard' under its prying eyes as the child custodian, rod in hand to smite (Gal. 3:23-25; 4:2), or 'the elements of the world' which held them 'in bondage' (Gal. 4:3), or false gods (Gal. 4:8), they were outside of Christ (Eph. 2:11-12), and 'under sin' (Gal. 3:22), 'committed... to disobedience' (Rom. 11:32), trapped in 'the snare of the devil, having been taken captive by him to do his will' (2 Tim. 2:26), under the wrath of God (John 3:36; Eph. 2:1-3), condemned already (John 3:18).

But, having believed, having come to Christ, they have been liberated from all such slavery and misery, having died to the law (Rom. 7:4-6; Gal. 2:19-20). As the apostle declares: 'You were the slaves of sin yet you... [have] been set free' (Rom. 6:17-18). How many scriptures speak of this rest, this liberty, this freedom from sin, law and death, this ceasing from works! Here is but a selection:

If you abide in my word, you are my disciples indeed. And you shall know the truth, and the truth shall make you free... Therefore if the Son makes you free, you shall be free indeed... It is finished (John 8:31-32,36; 19:30).
We have peace with God through our Lord Jesus Christ... Reckon yourselves to be dead indeed to sin, but alive to God in Christ Jesus our Lord... Sin shall not have dominion over you, for you are not under law but under grace... But God be thanked, that though you were slaves of sin, yet you obeyed from the heart that form of doctrine to which you were delivered. And having been set free from sin, you became slaves of righteousness... But now having been set free from sin, and having become slaves of God, you have your fruit to holiness, and the end everlasting life... For you did not receive the spirit of bondage again to fear, but you received the Spirit of adoption by whom we cry out: 'Abba, Father'... Who shall bring a charge against God's elect? It is God who justifies. Who is he who condemns? It is Christ who died, and furthermore is also risen, who is even at the right hand of God, who also makes intercession for us... Now may the God

of hope fill you with all joy and peace in believing, that you may abound in hope by the power of the Holy Spirit (Rom. 5:1; 6:11,14,17-18,22; 8:15,33-34; 15:13).
God has called us to peace (1 Cor. 7:15).
Now the Lord is the Spirit; and where the Spirit of the Lord is, there is liberty (2 Cor. 3:17).
So then, brethren, we are not children of the bondwoman but of the free. For freedom Christ has made us free... For you, brethren, have been called to liberty (Gal. 4:31; 5:1,13).
[Christ] himself is our peace... making peace... And he came and preached peace (Eph. 2:14-17).

In short, instead of labouring under the old covenant, in bondage to sin, the flesh and the law, the believer in Christ is in the new covenant, free, at liberty, at peace, enjoying ease of conscience, knowing he is perfectly sinless in the sight of God, beyond all risk of condemnation (Rom. 5:1; 8:1; Eph. 5:25-27; Heb. 10:14). And he *rests* in it.[146]

I know I repeat myself, and that this annoys some, but I cannot refrain here. This glorious truth needs to be shouted from the rooftops. The believer has ceased from his own works. He has come to rest in Christ. Instead of keeping the weekly sabbath as a shadow of true rest, he enjoys real rest in Christ, he enjoys a permanent peace with God. He has the Spirit, the one who, removing his fear and bearing witness with his spirit, assures him that he belongs to Christ (Rom. 8:14-17,23; 2 Cor. 1:21-22; 5:5; Gal. 4:6-7; Eph. 1:13-14; 4:30; 1 John 2:20-27; 3:24; 4:13; 5:6,9-11). He has died to the law, the killing letter, the condemning ministry of the law, and he is alive in Christ, he is alive by the Spirit (Rom. 7:4-6; 8:2; 2 Cor. 3:6-9; Gal. 2:19; 5:18).[147] And he rests in this assurance, because he rests in the Lord Jesus.

I say to all believers reading your book: 'It is for freedom that Christ has set us free. Stand firm, then, and do not let yourselves be burdened again by a yoke of slavery' (Gal. 5:1).

And I would address all men, not just believers: Listen to Christ. Hear what he offers in the new covenant:

---

[146] See my *Four 'Antinomians' Tried and Vindicated*, Brachus, 2013. I am not, of course, teaching sinless perfection. But the believer is utterly beyond condemnation in Christ.
[147] See my *Assurance*.

Come to me, all you who labour and are heavy laden [who work to exhaustion, NASB margin], and I will give you rest. Take my yoke upon you and learn from me... and you will find rest for your souls. For my yoke is easy and my burden is light (Matt. 11:28-30).

This is the glory of the new covenant: 'For I have satiated the weary soul, and I have replenished every sorrowful soul' (Jer. 31:25), precious words written in the context of the new covenant (Jer. 31:31-34). This is true of every believer, now!

So much for the present sabbath. Think, for a moment, of the ultimate rest for the child of God; namely, the *eternal* sabbath. What must that be! Indescribable! This, too, is held out to us in Hebrews 4. Yes, although I reject the *limitation* of Hebrews 4 to the believer's eternal rest, nevertheless such a rest is guaranteed to every child of God:

Behold, a great multitude which no one could number, of all nations, tribes, peoples, and tongues, standing before the throne and before the Lamb, clothed with white robes, with palm branches in their hands, and crying out with a loud voice, saying: 'Salvation belongs to our God who sits on the throne, and to the Lamb!'... These are the ones who came out of the great tribulation, and washed their robes and made them white in the blood of the Lamb. Therefore they are before the throne of God, and serve him day and night in his temple. And he who sits on the throne will dwell among them. They shall neither hunger any more nor thirst any more; the sun shall not strike them, nor any heat, for the Lamb who is in the midst of the throne will shepherd them and lead them to living fountains of waters. And God will wipe away every tear from their eyes... And I heard a loud voice from heaven saying: 'Behold, the tabernacle of God is with men, and he will dwell with them, and they shall be his people, and God himself will be with them and be their God. And God will wipe away every tear from their eyes; there shall be no more death, nor sorrow, nor crying; and there shall be no more pain, for the former things have passed away'. Then he who sat on the throne said: 'Behold, I make all things new' (Rev. 7:9-10,14-17; 21:3-5).

And it will not only be the saints who enjoy this eternal rest or sabbath, 'for we know that the whole creation groans and labours with birth pangs until now'. And it does not groan in vain. It, too, will enjoy its sabbath, for 'the creation will be delivered from the bondage of corruption into the glorious liberty of the children of

God' (Rom. 8:18-23), when 'mortality' shall 'be swallowed up by life' (2 Cor. 5:1-6). For:

The wolf also shall dwell with the lamb, the leopard shall lie down with the young goat, the calf and the young lion and the fatling together; and a little child shall lead them. The cow and the bear shall graze; their young ones shall lie down together; and the lion shall eat straw like the ox. The nursing child shall play by the cobra's hole, and the weaned child shall put his hand in the viper's den. They shall not hurt nor destroy in all my holy mountain, for the earth shall be full of the knowledge of the LORD as the waters cover the sea (Isa. 11:6-9).

Consequently, as believers: 'We, according to his promise, look for new heavens and a new earth in which righteousness dwells' (2 Pet. 3:13).

It is true, of course, that 'eye has not seen, nor ear heard, nor have entered into the heart of man the things which God has prepared for those who love him. But God has revealed them to us through his Spirit' (1 Cor. 2:9-10). What are these 'things'? Such things as these:

And there shall be no more curse, but the throne of God and of the Lamb shall be in it, and his servants shall serve him. They shall see his face, and his name shall be on their foreheads. And there shall be no night there: They need no lamp nor light of the sun, for the Lord God gives them light. And they shall reign for ever and ever (Rev. 22:3-6).

And all is in and through Christ: 'For it pleased the Father that in him all the fullness should dwell, and by him to reconcile all things to himself, by him, whether things on earth or things in heaven, having made peace through the blood of his cross' (Col. 1:19-20).

This is what the sabbath was teaching Israel in the old covenant – if only they had listened. That is, the law of Moses, all the law, including the ten commandments – specifically, the fourth, the sabbath – continually pointed the Jews to the fulfilment of all the shadows; namely, Christ and the glories he would bring in with the new covenant. All the prophets spoke of it (1 Pet. 1:8-12).[148] It was *rest* which the repeated sabbath of the old covenant was pointing to. It was *rest in Christ* which the law and the prophets were constantly proclaiming – in every daily sacrifice, in every

---

[148] There are well over 200 references to 'rest' in the Old Testament.

weekly sabbath, in all the sabbaths, in the settlement and enjoyment of the fruitful land of Canaan. Indeed, God had given a clear indication of it in his own rest after creation (Gen. 2:2; Heb. 4:3-4), and the promise of rest for Israel in Canaan (Heb. 3:7-19). Creator-rest, Canaan-rest and ceasing-rest typified Christ-rest for believers.

Sadly, the majority of Jews never understood this, nor did they enter into the spiritual meaning of their repeated observances, including and especially, the sabbath. They saw the shadow and clung to that – and frequently not even that! If only they had seen Christ, and trusted him, and entered the rest he offered! Some did; Abraham for one (John 8:56) – and many others (Hebrews 11). Grievously, the Jews, by and large, did not. The overwhelming mass of the Jews who left Egypt would not, could not, enter God's rest because of unbelief (Heb. 3:7-19). The failure was still prevalent in David's time (Ps. 95:7-11; Heb. 3:7-19; 4:1-8). The same goes for the time of Christ on earth: 'He came to his own, and his own did not receive him' (John 1:11). Christ would have gathered them, but they would not (Matt. 23:37; Luke 13:34; John 5:40).

But by God's grace, others did receive him (John 1:12). In words pregnant with meaning, 'Simeon.. this man... just and devout', who was 'waiting for the consolation of Israel, and the Holy Spirit was upon him', on seeing and holding the Christ, 'blessed God and said':

Lord, now you are letting your servant depart in peace, according to your word; for my eyes have seen your salvation which you have prepared before the face of all peoples, a light to bring revelation to the Gentiles, and the glory of your people Israel (Luke 2:25-32).

This is true of all who receive Christ, and enter into rest by him. 'There remains therefore a rest for the people of God', which rest is entered by faith in Christ. 'Let us therefore be diligent to enter that rest' (Heb. 3:12-15; 4:1-11).[149]

---

[149] This is not salvation by works. The writer is making it clear that we must have all our hope fixed on Christ alone, we must abide in him, and never drift away from him. We must never allow ourselves to have any old-covenant shadow imposed on us (Col. 2:16-17), which, with respect,

In light of all this, how can anybody think that the inspired writer would have encouraged believers, in such strong terms, to make sure they did not falter on the weekly sabbath! The notion is risible! The believer, having the reality in Christ, has no need of the shadow. He has Christ. And Christ is all (Col. 3:11).[150]

Listen to Calvin on Hebrews 4. He was clear that the writer:

Designedly alluded to the sabbath in order to reclaim the Jews[151] from its external observances; for in no other way could its abrogation be understood, except by the knowledge of its spiritual design. He then treats of two things together; for by extolling the excellency of grace, he stimulates us to receive it by faith, and in the meantime he shows us in passing what is the true design of the sabbath, lest the Jews[152] should be foolishly attached to the outward rite. Of its abrogation indeed he does [not] expressly speak, for this is not his subject, but by teaching them that the rite had a reference to something else, he gradually withdraws them from their superstitious notions. For he who understands that the main object of the precept was not external rest or earthly worship, immediately perceives, by looking on Christ, that the external rite was abolished by his coming; for when the body appears, the shadows immediately vanish away. Then our first business always is to teach that Christ is the end of the law.

As one hymn writer expressed it:[153]

> *The sabbath day, that day of rest,*
> *Was sanctified and blest*
> *To point us to our Saviour Christ,*
> *In whom alone is rest.*

Iain, is precisely what you are trying to do. As for the eternal element of this 'rest', the believer must persevere, as Hebrews tells us repeatedly (Heb. 4:1,11; 6:4-8; 10:19-30; 11:1-40; 12:1-29; *passim*).

[150] Take Christ's discourse on the manna (John 6:30-58). The message is plain: Do not cling to the shadow; look for the reality, Christ; cling to him. As I say, bearing in mind Ex. 16:1-35; Neh. 9:13-15, there is a powerful parallel with the sabbath.

[151] What Calvin says fits present-day sabbatarians like a glove.

[152] As previous note.

[153] Don Fortner ('Christ Is My Sabbath Rest', donfortner.com); the cover of *New Focus*, Go Publications, Eggleston, August/September 1999, Vol.4 No.2.

That legal sabbath ended when
Christ died and rose again;
Yet there's a sabbath that remains,
A rest that's found in him.

'Come unto me', the Saviour said,
'And I will give you rest'.
O weary sinners, cease from works,
Trust Christ and find sweet rest.

Ah, sweet refreshment for my soul,
The rest of faith is rest!
Ceasing from works, I trust God's Son –
Christ is my sabbath rest!

And as Joseph Hart put it:

To all God's people now remains a sabbatism, [154]
A rest from pains,
And works of slavish kind;
When tired with toil, and faint through fear,
The child of God can enter here,
And sweet refreshment find.

To this, by faith he oft retreats;
Bondage and labour quite forgets,
And bids his cares adieu;
Slides softly into promised rest,
Reclines his head on Jesus' breast,
And proves the sabbath true.

This, and this only, is the way,
To rightly keep the sabbath day.
Which God has holy made.
All keepers that come short of this,
The substance of the sabbath miss,
And grasp an empty shade. [155]

---

[154] 'Sabbatism'. Hart clearly spotted the significant change the writer to the Hebrews made in Heb. 4:9. He had been using *katapausis* and *katapauō* ('rest', noun and verb), and doing so frequently, but changed to *sabbatismos*, 'a keeping sabbath, the blessed rest from toils and troubles', the only time the word is used in Scripture.

[155] Joseph Hart: *Hart's Hymns*, Old Paths Gospel Press, Choteau, 1965, number 31; Gadsby: *Hymns* number 358; *Gospel Hymns* number 1026.

Iain, I hope this goes some way towards explaining why I say your talk of 'an element of truth' is grudging. By using such a phrase, you are playing down one of the greatest glories of the new covenant; indeed, you are demeaning it. You are diminishing one of the greatest privileges God grants his people here and now.[156]

Let me quote from two Anabaptists to bring this section to a close. I start with Melchior Hofmann, one who rightly maintained that 'all the promises of God tend... [to] that [which]... all... victors [in] the true kingdom of God [receive] here and now as their inheritance; [namely,] that the same enter into the holy [of holies] and come to the sabbath and the true rest'.[157]

And Sebastian Franck:

From the moment when the sabbath, circumcision and the commandment concerning the temple and offerings have been abrogated [literally, cut off], God recognises them no longer as his ordinances, although they were hitherto expressly ordained, and says [Isa. 1:10ff]: What concern are the temple and sacrifices to me? I am full of burnt offerings... The Spirit of God is alone the teacher of the new covenant... And just as the church is today a purely spiritual thing, so also is all law, promise, reward, spirit, bread, wine, sword, kingdom, life – all [are] in the Spirit and no longer outward.[158]

Such is the way, I repeat, for believers to read the old covenant in general. Can you not hear the echoes of 'letter' and 'Spirit', to which I have already referred? And, in regard to perhaps what is the greatest bone of contention over the law – the keeping of the sabbath – this is the vital principle of interpretation.

In short, there is no weekly sabbath for the believer. The Lord's day is not 'the Christian sabbath'. Not at all! The believer's

---

[156] For more, see my 'Sabbath'; 'Sabbath Rest For Believers'; 'Christ The Believer's Sabbath' (sermonaudio.com).
[157] Melchior Hofmann: *The Ordinance of God* (1530) in *Spiritual and Anabaptist Writers: Documents Illustrative of the Radical Reformation*, edited by George Huntston Williams, SCM Press Ltd., London, 1957, pp190-191.
[158] Sebastian Franck: *A Letter to John Campanus* (1531), in *Spiritual and Anabaptist Writers: Documents Illustrative of the Radical Reformation*, edited by George Huntston Williams, SCM Press Ltd., London, 1957, pp149-150.

sabbath is not confined to a mere 24 hours. It does not consist of a day which is shrouded in 'complications' (your word), a day which he has to try to make 'bright' (again, your word). No! The believer enjoys a permanent, continual and unending sabbath: Christ.

Conclusion

When talking about a day of the week, believers should not call it 'the sabbath'. It is not! The sabbath, as it concerns a day of the week, was a Jewish day, an old-covenant concept, and does not belong to the Christian. It did not belong to all men indiscriminately; it does not belong to all men today; it belonged only to the Jews; it has now been abolished in Christ since he is the true sabbath. If only this was understood and acted upon! It would save any amount of trouble and confusion. Too many Reformed people try to apply the fourth commandment to believers in a semi old-covenant, letter-ridden way. With respect, Iain, you do! Since they are under the new covenant, however, believers should no more keep the sabbath than they should sacrifice, set up priests, build a temple, or keep the Passover.

Not only that. When they use these old covenant words, believers should do as the New Testament, and use them to convey a spiritual meaning only. Christ is our Passover; Christ is our priest; Christ is our sacrifice; Christ is our altar; Christ is our sabbath. Christ is all (Col. 3:11).

Iain, *this is the point of all this discussion*. The observance of the sabbath *is* a matter of life and death – not in the sense you mean, however. Unless a sinner finds true sabbath rest in this life, he will perish eternally.

With that thought throbbing within me, I turn to all who read these pages. There is a sabbath for sinners. It is Christ. Christ is the only resting place for sinners. Christ is the only resting place for you. Unless you are in Christ, you will perish. Come to Christ, then, and come now, and you will be 'in Christ'. But you only come 'into Christ' by trusting him for salvation. Unless you are born again, you will never enter the kingdom, or even see it. Unless you have repented and are trusting Christ, you are even now in your sins, under the wrath of God, and struggling to earn your salvation, vainly striving to be right with God. Give it up! Lay down your arms! Come to Christ and enter into rest! Come now!

Listen to Jesus:

Come to me, all you who are weary and burdened, and I will give you rest. Take my yoke upon you and learn from me, for I am gentle and humble in heart, and you will find rest for your souls. For my yoke is easy and my burden is light (Matt. 11:28-30).

More than listen to Jesus. Believe his promise. More than believe his promise. Trust him. Come to him, I plead with you, and, on the authority of God's word, I assure you that will receive his promised rest.

Appendices

Appendix 1

Adam and the fourth commandment

As I said in the main body of the book, there now follows an excursus, enlarging on the point that if you, Iain, are right – and Adam was given the fourth commandment – he must, as a consequence, have been given all ten. Just to explain that when, in what follows, I say: 'I will return to something', I am assuming that this excursus is being read at the appropriate point in the book.

I admit that you nowhere state explicitly that God gave Adam the ten commandments – although, as you know, many Reformed teachers are not shy about asserting it. But if Adam was given a commandment to observe the sabbath, as you claim he was, what else could it be, other than the fourth of the ten? Moreover, you are very clear: 'There is a unity to the moral law [in your terms, the ten commandments]. Like a sheet of glass, if broken at one point, the whole is shattered'.[1] I am sure you will agree that if Adam was given the fourth commandment, he must have been given the ten. God did not shatter the pane of glass into ten shards, and give one of them to Adam, did he?

Indeed, when you come to the episode of the manna (Exodus 16),[2] you are prepared to state that it had been 'thousands of years' before Sinai that God had given the Israelites 'direction regarding the seventh day'. You continue:

Nothing in Exodus 16 suggests that the appointment of a special seventh day of rest was only now being introduced. Had the manna miracle of Exodus 16 followed the giving of the ten commandments in Exodus 20, we would have understood the fourth commandment as the foundation for the 'test' [in question]... When we come to the wording of the fourth commandment, its language confirms that the

---

[1] Murray p150.
[2] See below.

sabbath was not new but already existing... The appointment of the day of rest comes from the time of creation.[3]

In saying this, you are clearly linking the fourth commandment with the so-called commandment given to Adam.

That is not all. When you go on to speak of 'a fuller teaching on the sabbath' at Sinai – I will return to this gloss in the body of the book – you are in effect saying that Adam had been given the fourth commandment, at least in its essentials.

What is more, you are explicit:

If the case we [that is, I (IHM)] have given from Genesis 2:3 is sound,[4] then it is already clear that the fourth commandment does not belong exclusively to the Jews.[5]

This can only mean that in Adam all men were given the fourth commandment. Adam, in particular, was given it.

Again, by your reference, in connection with the sabbath,[6] to Romans 2:15 – even though you get this verse completely wrong[7] – you show that you think all men by nature have the law of God (in your terms, the ten commandments) written within them. Moreover, you explicitly say that 'all men by nature' are 'under law', and you clearly mean the law of God (in your terms, the ten commandments).[8] What is more, when you speak of the natural man's 'obligation' to keep the sabbath, you allege that this obligation:

...rests upon the eternal principles set out in the moral law [the ten commandments, in your terms]. Fallen man can, of himself, keep none of the ten commandments truly, yet he is still held to account for the obedience which God requires. Man's hostility to the fourth commandment is part of the antagonism with which he reacts to God

---

[3] Murray pp144-147. I admit the last clause is part of a sentence which begins with 'if' but you are clearly asserting that you are convinced there is no 'if' about it.

[4] And you clearly think it is. You are really saying: 'Since my case is sound...'.

[5] Murray p148.

[6] Murray p149.

[7] See below, in the body of the book.

[8] Murray p157.

himself (Rom. 8:7)... The moral law [the ten commandments, in your terms] exists for mankind.[9]

You had already posed the question: 'If the fourth commandment is to be considered redundant, and no longer part of the moral law of God, why is it that the New Testament, in repeated references to man's continued obligation to the law,[10] makes no exception?' And you had thereby deduced: 'The moral law... has authority over Gentile as well as Jew (Rom. 2:15)'.[11]

Hence, once again, on your system, in Adam all men must have been given the ten commandments. Adam, in particular, was.

Yet again, you quote Calvin with approval who, when he was talking about the sabbath, said that God:

...instructs us what we are to do... We have a God who is resting to be [that is, in his rest, he gives us] a mirror and pattern so that we may conform ourselves to him... Help will come to us from the day itself which is given to us, during which we abandon all occupations, all worldly cares and thoughts, in order to give our minds to that holy meditation we mentioned... Now in the law, God commanded the day of rest for another reason, and at this point we must carefully distinguish between the order God established in the creation of the world and this commandment which appears in the law of Moses... to give another and differing view; namely, that it is a shadow and figure of spiritual rest... But the fact remains that we have one definite day of the week... There are two facets of observance... God continued in the law what he had begun at the creation of the world... So let us learn to sanctify the day of rest in order to bring ourselves into conformity with our God's example and preserve the order which he established to be inviolable till the end.

And so on.[12] If this does not mean that Adam and Moses were given the same law, but Moses was given an additional supporting reason (echoes of your 'fuller') for the observance of the sabbath, words have lost all meaning.

---

[9] Murray p166.

[10] Would you give us the New Testament passages which make these 'repeated references to man's continued obligation', please?

[11] Murray p149.

[12] Murray pp150-152.

In short, you really do think that in Adam all men were given the ten commandments. Adam, in particular, was.

Now this, of course, must include all the punishments for breaking those commandments. After all, nobody can miss the highly negative cast of those commands.[13] The fact is, punishment for lack of obedience is a fundamental principle of the law, any law, law in general, the law of God in particular: 'You must obey my laws and be careful to follow my decrees. I am the LORD your God. Keep my decrees and laws, for the man who obeys them will live by them' (Lev. 18:4-5); 'Moses describes in this way the righteousness that is by the law: "The man who does these things will live by them"' (Rom. 10:5). Clearly, the man who does not obey the law will not live. Israel knew full well what God wanted. They detected and felt the iron fist in the velvet glove when God declared: 'Oh, that their hearts would be inclined to fear me and keep all my commands always, so that it might go well with them and their children forever!' (Deut. 5:29). Just in case it needs pointing out, when the Israelites were told that obedience would mean things would go well for them, they were being warned that disobedience would carry a heavy penalty. The truth is, God would never give a command without setting out the promise for obedience, and the curse for disobedience. Repeated curses for disobedience to the law are written plain across Scripture, right from the giving of the law at Sinai (Ex. 20:5,7; 21:17; Deut. 27:11-26; Gal. 3:10).[14]

Thus, on your argument, you really do believe that Adam was given the ten commandments, warnings and all. In the body of the book, I deal with some of the many consequences and illogicalities which stem from this remarkable and mistaken assertion. It further means, of course, that Adam was given all 613 commandments of

---

[13] Apart from their general tone, see the repeated: 'You shall not... but if you do...' (Ex. 20:4-11). In fact, as Paul tells us (Eph. 6:2), only one of the ten commandments is couched in terms of a promise.

[14] The same goes for the gospel. For example: 'Believe on the Lord Jesus, and you will be saved' (Acts 16:31). 'He who believes in him is not condemned; but he who does not believe is condemned already, because he has not believed in the name of the only begotten Son of God' (John 3:18).

the law. As you yourself state, the law[15] is a sheet of glass, a sheet that cannot be broken.[16] I know that you (along with nearly all the Reformed) like to break the sheet into three, but this convenient trick cannot stand scrutiny.[17]

In short, you do believe that Adam was given the ten commandments; you have to, otherwise, as you realise, the wheel falls off. Worse, the bottom falls out of your argument, leaving it to sink without trace. As you say, unless Adam was given the sabbath, then the sabbath only ever applied to the Jews.

---

[15] You try to limit this to 'the moral law'. We really must have **scriptural** *proof* of this manifestly false position.
[16] Murray p150.
[17] See my *Christ* pp100-104,392-400.

Appendix 2

The sabbath the old-covenant sign for Israel

I devote this Appendix to the fact that God gave the sabbath to Israel as a special distinguishing marker, separating them from all other nations. I do so because this principle encapsulates most, if not all, the scriptural teaching which shows us that the sabbath stood or fell with Israel's role in the old covenant. Consequently, Iain, you are utterly out of order to teach sabbatarianism today. The sabbath fell with Israel, fell with the old covenant, because it had been fulfilled and therefore rendered obsolete in and through the finished work of Christ.

Let me prove it.

We know that Israel, and Israel alone, out of all the nations, was privileged to be given God's law through Moses on Sinai. We have an abundance of scriptures which put it beyond doubt (Deut. 4:1 – 6:25; Ps. 147:19-20; Rom. 3:1-2; 9:4-5, and so on). In this, Israel was unique among all the nations.

He has revealed his word to Jacob, his laws and decrees to Israel. He has done this for no other nation; they do not know his laws (Ps. 147:19-20).
What advantage, then, is there in being a Jew, or what value is there in circumcision? Much in every way! First of all, they have been entrusted with the very words of God (Rom. 3:1-2).
[Consider] the people of Israel. Theirs is the adoption as sons; theirs the divine glory, the covenants, the receiving of the law, the temple worship and the promises. Theirs are the patriarchs, and from them is traced the human ancestry of Christ, who is God over all, forever praised! Amen (Rom. 9:4-5).

Comment is surely superfluous. Israel was given the law; Israel alone, of all the nations, was given the law; the law was given to Israel for Israel and for no others. This, at a stroke, destroys universal sabbatarianism in particular, and Calvin's threefold use of the law in general.

If you respond by asking if the same goes for the other laws, I say: 'Yes!' The basic ground upon which Scripture condemns pagans is not their breaking the law of God – which they were never given. It is that they suppress, warp, ignore and deny the light of nature and conscience, the light that God has placed in every man:

The wrath of God is being revealed from heaven against all the godlessness and wickedness of men who suppress the truth by their wickedness, since what may be known about God is plain to them, because God has made it plain to them. For since the creation of the world God's invisible qualities – his eternal power and divine nature – have been clearly seen, being understood from what has been made, so that men are without excuse. For although they knew God, they neither glorified him as God nor gave thanks to him, but their thinking became futile and their foolish hearts were darkened... Furthermore, since they did not think it worthwhile to retain the knowledge of God, he gave them over to a depraved mind, to do what ought not to be done... Although they know God's righteous decree that those who do such things deserve death, they not only continue to do these very things but also approve of those who practice them...

God does not show favouritism. All who sin apart from the law will also perish apart from the law, and all who sin under the law will be judged by the law. For it is not those who hear the law who are righteous in God's sight, but it is those who obey the law who will be declared righteous. (Indeed, when Gentiles, who do not have the law, do by nature things required by the law, they are a law for themselves, even though they do not have the law, since they show that the requirements of the law are written on their hearts, their consciences also bearing witness, and their thoughts now accusing, now even defending them). This will take place on the day when God will judge men's secrets through Jesus Christ, as my gospel declares (Rom. 1:18-21,28,32; 2:11-16).

Of course, more light brings increased responsibility and greater condemnation. But, as the above extracts prove, all men have enough light in nature and conscience to hold them accountable to God.

By the way, the fact that only Israel had the law ought to signal an end to Reformed preparationism.[1] The Jews, of course, having been given the law, were blameworthy for their disobedience to it. But God will never condemn non-Jews for not obeying a law they

---

[1] See my *Christ* pp pp51-61,127-140,348-358,420-430.

have not been given; namely, the Mosaic law. The Gentiles, of course, have the light of Romans 2:14-15. Consequently, since they knew that the Gentiles did not have the law, no biblical preachers ever used the law when addressing pagans.

Now let me come to the particular: the sabbath was God's special sign for Israel and only Israel.

Although God could say: 'All the earth is mine', he chose to declare to the Israelites: 'You shall be a special treasure to me above all people'. But there was a condition: 'Now therefore, *if* you will indeed obey my voice and keep my covenant, *then* you shall be a special treasure to me above all people' (Ex. 19:5). 'Keep my covenant'; in other words: 'Keep my law'. In giving this new nation – this nation of Israel, his nation – his law in order to mark them out as his people, in particular God gave them a special – unique – sign that they were his people. This sign belonged to no other people, since only Israel was his nation. And this sign was his sabbaths: 'Moreover I also gave them my sabbaths, to be a sign between them and me, that they might know that I am the LORD who sanctifies them' (Ezek. 20:12); that is, separates them from all other peoples. God commanded the Jews 'to hallow my sabbaths, and they will be a sign between me and you, that you may know that I am the LORD your God' (Ezek. 20:20). And the same applied to their following generations (Ex. 31:13). By 'sabbaths', of course, God meant the weekly sabbaths in particular. In short, God commanded the Hebrew people from that time on to keep his law – including the sabbath – especially the sabbath – *and especially the sabbath as a sign that they were God's nation, distinct from all others*:

Surely my sabbaths you shall keep, for it is a sign between me and you throughout your generations, that you may know that it is the LORD who sanctifies you. You shall keep the sabbath, therefore, for it is holy to you. Everyone who profanes it shall surely be put to death... Work shall be done for six days, but the seventh is the sabbath of rest, holy to the LORD. Whoever does any work on the sabbath day, he shall surely be put to death. Therefore the children of Israel shall keep the sabbath, to observe the sabbath throughout their generations as a perpetual covenant. It is a sign between me and the children of Israel for ever; for in six days the LORD made the heavens and the earth, and on the seventh day he rested and was refreshed (Ex. 31:13-17).

Incidentally, the time when Israel became a nation[2] is vitally connected with this business of the law, and the sabbath in particular. It confirms that the law was given only to the nation of Israel, not to Adam, not to the Gentiles. The sabbath was introduced to the new nation in the wilderness at the giving of the manna (Exodus 16), and within a few short weeks it was heavily reinforced and set in stone at Sinai (Exodus 20). The sabbath was given to Israel, and only Israel, as the special marker that they were God's people. The people, receiving this sign of the sabbath, in conjunction with the rest of the law, promised their obedience as God's holy nation, and did so both before Sinai: 'Then all the people answered together and said, "All that the LORD has spoken we will do"' (Ex. 19:8), and after: 'Moses came and told the people all the words of the LORD and all the judgments. And all the people answered with one voice and said: "All the words which the LORD has said we will do"' (Ex. 24:3).

The tables of the law were housed in the special box constructed for the purpose – the ark of the covenant for Israel (Ex. 25:10,15-16; 40:19-20; Deut. 10:1-5; 1 Kings 8:9; Heb. 9:4), its name – 'the ark of the *covenant*' – pregnant with meaning. The commandments and the covenant were one (Ex. 34:28; Lev. 26:15; Deut. 4:13), symbolised by being one in the ark of the covenant. This holy box was placed at the very centre of the Jewish religion and nation. No hand was allowed to touch it – death fell upon the transgressor (2 Sam. 6:6-7). In this way, God was once again underlining the connection between the law and death (Rom. 7:9-10; 2 Cor. 3:6-7,9; Heb. 12:18-24). Moreover, he was signalling the status of the law as the separating marker for Israel.

Nor did the giving of the law stop in Exodus 20. The biblical record makes it very plain that God unfolded to the Jews a complete life-system involving worship, the family and society, to enable the fledgeling nation to run its affairs in a way which pleased God, distinct from all other peoples. So much so, how to deal with false worship and idolatrous altars (Ex. 20:22-26), how to manage servants (Ex. 21:2-11), recompense and retribution for personal injuries (Ex. 21:12-36), property laws (Ex. 22:1-31), the

---

[2] See my *Christ* pp27-37,337-341.

judicial system (Ex. 23:1-9), and the three annual feasts (Ex. 23:14-19) – all new revelation – were all made clear to Israel at this time of the formation of the nation.

Did you spot it? Did you spot the gap in the previous paragraph? I deliberately missed out one integral passage of Scripture in the list of new things the Lord made known to his people at that time. Indeed, I missed out the principal distinguishing mark of the old covenant. Which? When someone fills in an application form for a job, the prospective employer looks to see if there are any unexplained gaps. If there are, he attaches huge significance to them. What deliberate gap did I leave? Exodus 23:10-13. To what does this gap-passage refer? Sabbath laws! By omitting this, I tried to highlight the significance of the sabbath to the Jews at this time – it was part and parcel of the entire Jewish system of worship and daily life which was made known to them at the start of their existence as a nation. And it was the main marker to separate Israel from all other nations on earth.

After promising guidance and blessing for the nation, and commanding their obedience (Ex. 23:20-33), God then confirmed the covenant with Israel (Exodus 24). He went on to unfold other matters which had significance for the Jews and only them; namely, the tabernacle and all its concomitants, including the offerings and the priesthood (Exodus 25). As God drew his revelation to a close, he told the people through Moses that he had chosen and named two men to carry out the work (Ex. 31:1-11).

But there was one last piece of revelation needed to confirm the covenant in all its unique fullness for Israel. And what was that? It was the sabbath! 'Then the LORD spoke to Moses, saying':

Speak also to the Israelites saying: 'Surely my sabbaths you shall keep, for it is a sign between me and you throughout your generations, that you may know that it is the LORD who sanctifies you. You shall keep the sabbath, therefore, for it is holy to you. Everyone who profanes it shall surely be put to death... Work shall be done for six days, but the seventh is the sabbath of rest, holy to the LORD. Whoever does any work on the sabbath day, he shall surely be put to death. Therefore the children of Israel shall keep the sabbath, to observe the sabbath throughout their generations as a perpetual covenant. It is a sign between me and the children of Israel for ever' (Ex. 31:13-17).

Note the connection between the distinction (in that sense, the holiness) of the sabbath and the distinction (in that sense, the holiness) of the Israelites;[3] they stood or fell together in the covenant God made with the Hebrews at that time.

And after Israel's rebellion with the golden calf – after which God mercifully re-issued the covenant on Sinai – he repeated the process, giving Moses two new tablets of stone. In so doing, he restated his instructions pertaining to the covenant he was making with Israel, including warnings against idol worship, the keeping of the feasts, the redemption of the first-born, the sabbath and so on (Exodus 34). As God said: 'Write these words, for according to the tenor of these words I have made a covenant with you and with Israel' (Ex. 34:27). As Moses was addressing God just prior to this second visit to Sinai, he could rightly say of Israel: 'This nation is your people' (Ex. 33:13).

And upon Moses' return to the people, he went over the same ground as before: 'Then Moses gathered all the congregation of the children of Israel together, and said to them, "These are the words which the LORD has commanded you to do"'. Where did Moses begin? What was the *first* thing he put before the people? This:

Work shall be done for six days, but the seventh day shall be a holy day for you, a sabbath of rest to the LORD. Whoever does any work on it shall be put to death. You shall kindle no fire throughout your habitations on the sabbath day (Ex. 35:1-3).

---

[3] Iain, you say: 'The sabbath was also at this time [which time?] related to God's redemptive purposes. It was now a memorial not only of creation but of the nation's deliverance from Egypt (Deut. 5:15). The special day became a covenant sign of God's saving work in their midst (Ex. 31:16; Ezek. 20:12)' (Murray p147). In the body of the book, I have already referred to this. Let me now add that I detect your covenant theology, I am sorry to say. Naturally, I am not surprised. But the old-covenant redemption of Israel from Egypt was only a shadow of the believer's salvation in Christ in the new covenant. These two covenants are distinct; they are not different administrations of 'the covenant' – which, in the sense you use the phrase, does not exist in Scripture, but is an idea imposed upon it by Reformed covenant-theologians. Alas, it carries heavy penalties for those who adopt this theological template.

In other words, he began with the sabbath. Then followed instructions, as before, concerning the tabernacle, the men who would oversee the work, the priesthood and all the rest of it – all of which the Israelites carried out (Ex. 35:1 – 40:38). But I ask the question again: Where did God and Moses begin when restating God's covenant with Israel? With the sabbath!

All this would seem to be clarity itself; it would appear to settle the issue once and for all. The sabbath was given to the Jews. It was a Jewish day. The distinction (in that sense, holiness) of the day and the people stood or fell together. The sabbath was a mark – a unique sign – of God's covenant with them, and only with them. God did not give the sabbath to Adam. He did not give it to the Egyptians. He did not give it to the Edomites, Moabites, Ammonites... He gave it to the Hebrews. Indeed, as the Bible makes as clear as noonday, it is even more far-reaching than this. The Gentiles did not have the law. And therefore the Gentiles could not have had the sabbath. God has never said: 'I give my sabbath to the nations. I give my sabbath to the UK, America, Australia...' Any such suggestion utterly ruins the revealed concept of the sabbath as the special distinguishing marker for Israel, and for Israel only.

There is no room for doubt that the law in general was given to the Jews, and, in particular, the sabbath was the special sign God gave to the Jews to signify they were his people (Ex. 31:12-17; Ezek. 20:10-12,20). This is confirmed by the very terms of the fourth commandment: God pointed out to the Jews that it applied to 'your stranger who is within your gates' (Ex. 20:10). The fact that this needed to be stated proves that the commandment was not of universal application – it did not, after all, apply to the stranger who was *not* living among the Jews.[4]

Now the very essence of a sign is this: it is special. The sabbath must have been special to the nation of the Jews – it *must* have been – otherwise the whole point of the sabbath as a sign would have been lost.[5] If everybody had the day, if it was a creation ordinance applying to all men as men, inevitably it could not have been distinctive to the Jews, and consequently no sign at all. At a

---

[4] See my earlier remarks on Ex. 12:43-49.
[5] Compare Rev. 2:17.

stroke, those passages which speak of the day as a unique sign for the Jews as a nation are thus rendered void of meaning.

What is more, the sabbath lasted as long as the old covenant, and no longer; that is, as long as the sacrifices, the priesthood and all the rest. All are fulfilled and abolished in Christ, rendered obsolete by him (Rom. 10:4; 2 Cor. 3:6-11; Gal. 3:19,23-25; Eph. 2:14-15; Heb. 7:12,18-19,22; 8:6-13; 9:10; 10:15-18). To sacrifice now is to insult the blood of Christ; to keep the sabbath is to insult the rest he brought. In both cases, it would be clinging to shadows when the reality is at hand.

Iain, by applying the sabbath to non-Jews, you are driving a coach and horses through this vital biblical principle; namely, that the sabbath was a sign for the Jews, as long as the old covenant was in force. This necessarily means that it was uniquely a day for the Jews. By taking the line you do, you are effectively emptying the day of its important biblical significance for the nation of Israel.

Will you do the same for other signs? I refer to Genesis 17:11 with Romans 4:11, and Exodus 13:8-16.

Let me explain: Abraham 'received the sign of circumcision' (Gen. 17:11; Rom. 4:11) as the sign of God's covenant with him; that is, he was given a special indicator, a special marker, unique to him and his descendants; it was a sign for them and for them alone. If circumcision had been given to the entire human race, its uniqueness would, obviously, have been lost; its value as a sign would have been destroyed. The idea that circumcision could be a sign for Abraham and his descendants, and yet be given to all mankind, is simply ludicrous.[6]

Then again, at the very time of leaving Egypt, the Jews were given the Feast of Unleavened Bread, which they had to observe when they were settled in their land. This served as a sign:

And you shall tell your son in that day, saying: 'This is done because of what the LORD did for me when I came up out of Egypt'. It shall be as a sign and as a memorial between your eyes, that the LORD's law may be in your mouth; for with a strong hand the LORD has brought you out of Egypt (Ex. 13:8-9).

---

[6] Of course, the spiritual equivalent (which is regeneration – *not* baby sprinkling!) applies to all members of the new covenant; that is believers.

The Feast of Unleavened Bread was for the Jews, and only for the Jews. More, it was *a sign* for them, and for them alone. If all nations had been required to keep the feast, its very essence as a sign would have vanished. When God gave the Jews the Passover, he expressly forbade any foreigner to eat it (Ex. 12:43-49).

Then again, upon reaching Canaan the Jews had to redeem their first-born. By way of explanation, the father had to tell his son:

By strength of hand the LORD brought us out of Egypt, out of the house of bondage. And it came to pass, when Pharaoh was stubborn about letting us go, that the LORD killed all the first-born in the land of Egypt, both the first-born of man and animal. Therefore I sacrifice to the LORD all males that open the womb, but all the first-born of my sons I redeem.

As God said: 'It shall be as a sign on your hand and as frontlets between your eyes, for by strength of hand the LORD brought us out of Egypt' (Ex. 13:11-16). Once again, only the Jews were required to keep this service of redemption; it was a sign for them and them alone.

The same goes for the sabbath; it was a sign for the Jews, and it was therefore given specially and only to them. It has never belonged, as a day of observance, to any others.

All these old-covenant signs were given to the Israelites within three months of their leaving Egypt (Ex. 19:1). God instituted many new things for them at that time – all strange and unfamiliar to them; so much so they needed repeated instruction as to how they should behave; they simply did not know – it was all so new. God gave them a new calendar (Ex. 12:2); he gave them feasts which they had never known before (Ex. 12:1-28); he gave them a method of redemption – something not known before (Exodus 13); he gave them manna – something completely unknown on earth before (Exodus 16); he gave them a new judicial system (Exodus 18); he gave them his law, which involved a vast array of new things – a stated place to sacrifice, a stated, organised way of sacrifice, a stated priesthood, the tabernacle, the levitical system and so on (Exodus 19) – all utterly unknown before. God gave these things to the Jews as special signs and markers, laws, commands, statutes, regulations, ordinances, judgements and practices – practices which until that time in the wilderness, following Israel's exodus from Egypt, had never been known among men. Are we really to believe that one, and only one, of these special markers – the sabbath – the one great special sign for Israel, the one commandment specially picked out by God as a sign for them – *had* been known to all men for centuries? Are we asked to believe that the sabbath, the revelation of which comes slap bang in the middle of all the other new things revealed to the Jews, was not new? that it had been given to Adam (and thus to all men), thousands of years before? that it was a day for all men and not special to the Jews? I repeat my question: Did all these signs apply only to the Jews? Or do they all apply to all the human race for all time?

Of course not! They never did. They were given to the Jews for the Jews, in the old covenant. And they were all fulfilled, and therefore abolished, in Christ.

That the sabbath – along with the other signs – was for the Jews only is confirmed by the treatment of the sabbath in Nehemiah 9:13-15. On returning from exile, the levites led the Jews in praise of God, confession of their sin, and a renewal of the covenant (Neh. 9:5-38). And the fact that God, centuries before at Sinai, had made known his holy sabbath to them – the Jews – was an integral part of all this:

You came down also on Mount Sinai, and spoke with them from heaven, and gave them just ordinances and true laws, good statutes and commandments. You made known to them your holy sabbath, and commanded them precepts, statutes and law, by the hand of Moses your servant. You gave them bread from heaven for their hunger, and brought them water out of the rock for their thirst, and told them to go in to possess the land which you had sworn to give them.

There are several points. God made his sabbath known to the Jews, not to Adam: 'You made known to *them* your holy sabbath'. The Jews became Jews long after Adam's time. There were no Jews in Genesis 2. Again, it is expressly stated that God made his sabbath known in the wilderness (with the manna and then at Sinai) by Moses (Neh. 9:14); not in Eden, to Adam. Note also the way Nehemiah reversed the historical record – manna, sabbath, law – and made it law, sabbath, manna. Above all, notice how Nehemiah sandwiched the 'making known of the sabbath' between the revelation of the law on Sinai (Neh. 9:13), and the giving of the manna (Neh. 9:15). In short: God made known his holy sabbath to the Jews when he commanded them through Moses in the wilderness (Neh. 9:14), not when he himself rested at creation. Above all, God *made known* his sabbath at that time; he did not *remind* the Jews of a day which they had forgotten. This passage is utterly invincible!

It stands out a mile; Nehemiah 9:14 is conclusive: Israel did not have the sabbath or the law until God gave both law and sabbath to them in the Wilderness of Sin on their leaving Egypt. And he gave both to Israel, and to Israel alone. And when he gave the law (at Sinai), so soon after giving them the sabbath (in the desert), no wonder he told them to 'remember' it ; that is, to keep it, to observe it. It was the special marker, the special distinguishing sign for Israel in the old covenant, separating her from all other nations, and marking her as no other nation was ever to be marked. And it all fell, all was set aside, all became obsolete, defunct (Rom. 10:4; 2 Cor. 3:6-11; Eph. 2:14-15; Heb. 7:18-19; 8:13), with the finished work of Christ (John 19:30; Gal. 3:19). On all these counts, therefore, your call for national observance of the sabbath, today, and by all nations, is quite wrong.

One last time: the sabbath was the special marker, the distinguishing sign of the old covenant, and it applied to Israel, and to Israel only.

Christ is All: No Sanctification by the Law

Dr John S.Waldrip reviewed *Christ is All: No Sanctification by the Law*
*****Life changing!** July 20, 2013
David H.J.Gay writes in a way most can easily follow to show that an error concerning the Mosaic Law has found its way through Thomas Aquinas and John Calvin into mainstream Protestant thought. Gay shows the error of this and points the reader ever and always to the Lord Jesus Christ as the Object the divine Means by which the believer's sanctification is accomplished. I would give this book six stars if the author had left out the final chapter of the book.

Terence Clarke reviewed *Christ is All: No Sanctification by the Law*
*****Deals thoroughly with Christian sanctification in Christ rather than Moses (Law)** 16 August 2013
David Gay thoroughly deals with the biblical concept and application of sanctification (imparted righteousness) which he reveals is in Christ alone. He demolishes the teaching of the reformers and those that follow on this issue that sanctification is by the 10 Commandments. He shows that just as in justification Christ is all and as far as the sanctification of believers is concerned 'Christ is in all'. This is anything but an antinomian approach but emphasises the power of Christ in the Christian's life. David's style is unusual in that it displays a preacher's approach to delivery but is fresh and direct. He does repeat his arguments throughout the book so that the reader should be in no doubt of them or misunderstand them. He introduces briefly his amillennialist view on Israel which, I find, is not argued with the same biblical thoroughness as the main subject. Recommended for all those who have a true interest in biblical sanctification and the whole work of Christ.

Moe Bergeron reviewed *Christ is All: No Sanctification by the Law*
****At last a view of 'New Covenant' Sanctification** August 30, 2013
'Antinomian!' is a hideous charge that is levelled at those who do not believe in any use of Sinai's Law for the saint's sanctification. The fact of the matter is that anyone who subscribes to such a use, including a third use, of Sinai's Law denies the clear biblical teaching of Romans 7:6 and 2 Corinthians 3. The written code and the way of the Spirit are opposed to one another. In the apostle Peter's 2nd letter and in the 1st chapter he explains New Covenant sanctification. Learn of Christ! David Gay's work is a must read for all who understand that

the Lutheran/Reformed debate is not Law vs. Gospel. It truly is Letter vs. Spirit.

Mr Rod Angus reviewed *Christic is All: No Sanctification by the Law*
*****Insightful, courageous and clear** 27 August 2013
The Reformed teaching that the OT law, especially the 10 Commandments, is the Christian's standard and perfect rule for obedience, when not overtly taught, is nevertheless the incipient ingredient lurking in the minds of many believers. The belief that the Law is an aid to sanctification is a lie. The law dis-empowers and condemns, but never sanctifies. David Gay has written a unique book exposing this Reformed spell that has been cast over the Church. As he writes 'The same grace that saves... also sanctifies'. Grace wins the love of the heart in a way that the law never could. 'The Law of Christ' is 'a real law. Love is its goal, love is its motive'. My only real problem with David's wonderful book is his continued allegiance to the Augustine-Calvin Christologically deficient teaching on election. I have already contacted him over this, to which he graciously replied. I hope he sniffs this one out in the same way as he has exposed the lie concerning the believer and the law. Nevertheless, this is an outstanding piece of writing. Thank you David.

Amazon customer reviewed *Christ is All: No Sanctification by the Law*
*****Demolishes Reformed view of sanctification by law** November 12, 2013
Best and most thorough book on New Covenant Theology I have ever seen. Completely demolishes the erroneous Reformed doctrine of sanctification by law.

Tom Knotts reviewed *Christ is All: No Sanctification by the Law*
*****The best book I have ever read next to Bible on the law and grace** April 30, 2014
This book was recommended to me by my former pastor and I have to say it is the best book I have read on the law and grace. Gay takes the time to break each and every passage down dealing with the subject but the beauty is that he goes beyond that and ties in things I had never considered. A great book.

James M.Kray 'Lewis Fan' reviewed *Christ is All: No Sanctification by the Law*
*****So good, I read it 2 times in a row** June 27, 2014
A real challenge to the typical 'use the Law for your sanctification' view held in most Reformed circles. Very readable style too. I wonder how many are trapped in their doctrinal statements and/or confessions.

Have you ever noticed that Paul never says 'Walk in the Law'? and this by an ex-Pharisee! I bought the Kindle AND the paperback.

James M.Kray 'Lewis Fan' reviewed *Christ is All: No Sanctification by the Law*
*****A Very Good Presentation on Law/Gospel August 13, 2014
This book will get you thinking hard about the Law/Gospel relationship. If you are Reformed or think that the Law of Moses can be broken down into civil, ceremonial and moral, think again. Even non-Reformed have adopted this 3 way division. So good, I had to read it two times in a row.

Audio book: *Christ Is All: No Sanctification By The Law* (may be downloaded from sermonaudio.com)
JamesC. (Fallbrook, CA)
Great Audio Book! August 29, 2014
Thank you for providing this free audio book. I am benefiting greatly from the material in it. It is eye-opening – as radical as the biblical doctrine of election. I am seeing things that I once glossed over. Coming out of Way of the Master evangelism and Reformed thinking, the information in this book is causing a welcomed paradigm shift for me.

7407428R00061

Printed in Great Britain
by Amazon.co.uk, Ltd.,
Marston Gate.